Second Edition

The
Cultural
Experience

Ethnography in Complex Society

David W. McCurdy
Macalester College

James P. Spradley
late of Macalester College

Dianna J. Shandy
Macalester College

WAVELAND

PRESS, INC.

Long Grove, Illinois

To the memory of James P. Spradley

For information about this book, contact:
Waveland Press, Inc.
4180 IL Route 83, Suite 101
Long Grove, IL 60047-9580
(847) 634-0081
info@waveland.com
www.waveland.com

Printed in the United States of America

9 8 7 6 5

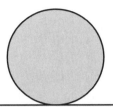

Contents

To the Instructor   vii

PART I: DOING ETHNOGRAPHY   1

1 Culture and Ethnography   3

Culture   5
  What Is Culture?   5
  Attributes of Culture   6
  Kinds of Culture   8

Ethnography   9
  What Is Ethnography?   9
  Naive Realism   9
  Ethnocentrism   10
  Subjects, Respondents, and Informants   10

2 Microcultures   13

What Are Microcultures?   13
Locating and Choosing a Microculture   16

3 Cultural Informants   21

Locating Cultural Informants   22
   Find an Informant You Already Know   22
   Find an Informant "Cold Turkey"   23
   Find an Informant through a Go-Between   23

Attributes of a Good Informant   25

One Informant or Many?   26

Identifying Yourself and Explaining the Project   27

Controlling Anxiety   28

Recording Ethnographic Field Data   28

Ethical Responsibilities   29
   Human Subjects Research Requirements   29

4 Discovering Folk Terms   33

The First Interview   34
   Explaining the Research   34
   Asking Descriptive Questions   35

Descriptive Questions   38

Field Notes   40

Preliminary Analysis   41

5 Discovering Taxonomic Structure   43

Taxonomic Structure   43
   Domains   43
   Taxonomies   44
   Semantic Relationships   46
   Design Principles of a Taxonomy   47

Eliciting Taxonomies   48
   Step 1: Analyzing Field Notes   48
   Step 2: Asking Structural Questions   50

Troubleshooting for Errors in Taxonomies   51
   Bad Spots   51
   Compound Taxonomies   52

Why Collect Taxonomies?   54

6 Discovering Meaning   57

Attributional Meaning   57

Discovering and Displaying Attributional Meaning   59
    Identifying Contrast Sets   59
    Constructing a Paradigm   60
    Checking for Attributes in Your Field Notes   61
    Asking Attribute Questions   63
    Culture or Personal Meaning?   65

7 Ethnographic Detail and Cultural Focus   67

Eliciting Ethnographic Detail   67

Focusing the Ethnography   74

8 Cultural Themes and Cultural Adaptation   77

Cultural Themes   77

Discovering Themes   79

Cultural Strategies   80

9 Writing and Using Ethnography   83

Writing the Ethnography   83
    Cultural Representation   84
    Writing and Ethics   85
    Audience   85
    Choosing a Thesis   86
    Parts of a Paper   87
    Using Taxonomies and Paradigms   90
    Using Quotes   91

Ethnographic Research and Uses   93
    Research Abroad   93
    Problem-Based Ethnography   93

Bibliography   97

PART II : STUDENT ETHNOGRAPHIES   101

**Getting the Truth:
The Police Detective and the Art of Interviewing**   103
    Cole Akeson

Juicing Their Way to the Top: Ethnography of a Tattoo Shop   112
    Jennifer Boehlke

No Money, No Honey: An Ethnography of Exotic Dancers   121
    Melissa Cowell

Where Did the Time Go?:
    A Look into a Jesuit Pastor's Struggle with Time   130
    Meghan Greeley

"Alice in Wonderland":
    The Culture of a Neighborhood Flower Shop   139
    Sana Haque

Dealing with Dickheads:
    An Ethnography of a Nightclub Staff Member   148
    John Hoch

Ethnography of a Legal Secretary   156
    Jordan Pender

Coping with Stress: An Ethnography of Firefighters   165
    Alex Rubenstein

The Modern Pest Control Revolution   172
    Byron Thayer

Catching Babies:
    An Ethnography of a Licensed, Traditional Midwife   179
    Natasha Winegar

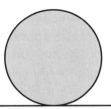

To the Instructor

What Is in the Second Edition?

When we introduced *The Cultural Experience* in 1972, we wrote, "This book is about ethnographic research for the undergraduate student." Despite the passing of many years, the evolution of cultural anthropology as a discipline, and restrictions on social research and the availability of willing informants, undergraduate ethnographic research remains the focus of this second edition. The new edition contains many of the features found in the original book. It asks students to choose a North American microculture (called a *cultural scene* in the first edition) to study. It invites students to find and locate a cultural informant. It teaches students to use methods associated with a single research approach, *ethnosemantics*, which focuses on interviewing. It uses a limited, cognitive definition of culture centering on the learned, shared knowledge that members of a group use to generate behavior and interpret experience. It also continues to contain student-authored ethnographies, all of which are new to this edition, to illustrate the ethnographic process and strategies for writing up results.

But there are also additions. The first part of the book that discusses the ethnographic method has been expanded from five to nine chapters. All have been written or rewritten to reflect experience gained from the supervision of nearly 6,000 student ethnographic projects over 33 years at Macalester College. There are now some boxed inserts that highlight problems and solutions to difficulties that may arise in the field. There is new material on how to use observation and narratives in the research process along with the ethnosemantic approach. There is greater emphasis on how to find cultural themes and adaptive challenges by analyzing ethnographic field data, and more extensive discussion of strategies to write the final ethnographic paper. Finally, there is an expanded treatment of ethical responsibilities toward informants including informed consent agreements, as well as a discussion of the significance of ethnographic research and its applications in the world of work.

Questions about Teaching Undergraduate Ethnographers

Over the years, colleagues have asked two important questions about our approach to undergraduate research: Can undergraduates who lack theoretical training do and learn from ethnographic research? Why does this book use a single approach, ethnosemantics, as the field method for undergraduate research instead of participant observation or other useful research strategies? Answers to these questions reveal something about our views on teaching through research and how these are reflected in the design of this book.

Can undergraduates conduct and learn from ethnographic research?

Given our experience with undergraduate research, we are sure the answer to this question is yes. Over the years we have been encouraged by the high quality of research produced by many of our undergraduates. In addition, numerous colleagues at other institutions report that they, too, have had their undergraduates do successful ethnographic research.

However, the question brings up a comparison that we think is worth mentioning. In the past, and we suspect even now, many anthropologists have argued that ethnographic research is best guided and organized by the identification of research problems and the use of anthropological theory. Since most undergraduates lack sufficient theoretical training or enough experience to identify significant problems, it follows that they can't easily design and carry out successful ethnographic field research.

Our answer to this problem now and in the past is to treat ethnography as a *discovery* process rather than a *theory-driven* process. In this book, we view culture as a system of knowledge shared by members of a group. Discovery ethnography is the process of uncovering, recording, and describing that knowledge. We often liken the discovery process to the experience of children who must learn their culture from parents, relatives, and other adults and children. Just like a school setting, informants become teachers, ethnographers become students.

One advantage of this approach is that children, and in our case undergraduate ethnographers, don't need theory or the identification of problems to learn a culture. They pick it up by watching and listening to other people. We believe a second advantage of discovery-oriented ethnography, which relates to a primary goal for most undergraduate instructors, is that undergraduates come away from the research process with a much deeper understanding of what culture means.

Why the focus on ethnosemantic interviewing?

Discovery ethnography may compensate for the theoretical insufficiency exhibited by most undergraduates, but even discovery ethnography must be organized in some way if students are to do successful work. We ignored this point when we first sent students out to do ethnography in the late 1960s. We asked them to find a group, ask questions, observe, and take notes. Students tried to meet these requirements, but they soon began to ask us questions: What should they look for when they observe? What questions should they ask? What should they do with the hodgepodge of material they collected? We found ourselves spending hours with each student in an effort to help with these questions. We were also discouraged to note that students tended to observe things and ask questions that reflected their own cultural backgrounds, preconceived notions of what a group was like, and personal interests. In short, they didn't know what to do, and much of what they did collect was shaped by ethnocentrism. Clearly the ethnographic task needed more structure.

To provide structure, we initially asked students to observe people in defined settings. For example, we sent students to watch the action in city and county courtrooms or had them choose public scenes such as a zoo gorilla house, difficult street crossing, or a Coke machine. Although students enjoyed their research and discovered some behavioral patterns, we still found that they often described the activities they witnessed from their own cultural viewpoints. We felt we needed to find a method that permitted informants, the *actors being observed*, to express what was going on from their own, inside, point of view.

We began to solve this problem by looking at our own field research experience. Ethnographic fieldwork held a powerful place in our own development as anthropologists. The field experience gave us a "cross-cultural" or "ethnographic" sense we were unable to achieve by reading books or viewing films. But our ethnographic success, if such occurred, depended on long-term immersion in a group as participant observers. Just like children, we learned the culture of a group by being in it, asking questions, and trying to act properly. But long-term field immersion was not an option for our undergraduates. They required a field method that would have some of the benefits of long-term ethnographic research but could be learned and used in one-semester courses or even as only part of a course.

We settled on the approach called *ethnosemantics*, or ethnoscience as it was often called. Generated in the late 1950s and 1960s, ethnosemantics was built on the idea that culture is learned, shared knowledge, much of which is coded in language. Anthropologists had always sought to learn their informants' languages and discovered much about the cultures they studied as a result. Ethnosemantics presented a more formal and structured approach to this process, and it was this method, rather than many other valuable anthropological field techniques, we found was the most useful and effective way to teach our students the concept of culture and the task of ethnography. This book is structured on that premise.

Acknowledgments

We wish to express our gratitude to the students of Macalester College over the past thirty years for their contributions, challenges, and conscientious pursuit of "the insider perspective." Each successive wave of students has taught us more about the ethnographic enterprise, identifying problems, and inventing solutions. Their experiences and ideas have been essential to the development of the approach presented in this book.

We wish especially to thank the ten authors whose ethnographic papers appear in this volume. They not only withstood our queries and suggestions in the classroom, they returned to edit their original papers for inclusion in this volume.

This book would not have been written without the original impetus of James P. Spradley. His collaboration with David McCurdy on the 1972 edition of *The Cultural Experience: Ethnography in Complex Society* is the foundation on which this new edition is based. We are also indebted to Jim's wife, Barbara Spradley, for her gracious support of this revised second edition.

Our editor at Waveland Press, Tom Curtin, was a patient and persistent force in moving this project to completion. Cole Akeson, author of the ethnographic paper on police detectives included in Part II of this book, was an invaluable editorial assistant in preparing parts of this volume for publication. His work on this project was supported by a grant from the W. M. Keck Foundation Student-Faculty Collaborative Research Program at Macalester College. We are grateful to Professor Ann Cottrell, San Diego State University, for her thoughtful comments on how ethnographic methods texts inform her teaching.

Finally, we would like to thank Carolyn McCurdy and David and Rhetta Power for their patience and support during this project.

PART I

DOING ETHNOGRAPHY

Culture and Ethnography

In 1961, an anthropologist, accompanied by an Indian assistant, drove his jeep over a rough dirt road to reach a village located in the hill country of southern Rajasthan, India. When he arrived there he saw a valley with scattered mud- and dung-plastered stone houses, a few dogs, and several men sitting and drinking from ceramic cups on the mud-plastered verandah of a small house by the road. He spoke few words of the local language. He did not know how to greet people, who the men were, or even how to ask questions.

Nevertheless, with the help of his associate and several visits, he received permission to build a bamboo house with the villagers' aid and to live in the community for a year and a half. By the end of that time, he learned the language well enough to manage daily conversation and greet people properly. He discovered that the house by the road was a *hotel* (tea stall) and that the men were drinking *chai*, a hot mixture of tea, milk, sugar, and several spices. He learned that the *gaon* (village) was divided into *phalla* (wards), that it had a *gameti* (headman), an informal but effective political and legal structure, and people who believed in a bewildering variety of gods, goddesses, and other supernatural beings. He discovered in detail the complex structure of kin identities and groups that organized people's social lives, and the many strategies villagers used to make a living. He learned how people conceived of the world and their place in it, and how to act in the little ways that guided day-to-day life in the community. In short, he was a typical anthropologist conducting an ethnographic field study. His goal was to learn the culture of the community, to discover what one needed to know in order to act and react like the people who lived there, to see the world as they conceived of it. His final goal was to return home and describe what he had learned in a way that his U.S. compatriots could understand. In short, he was doing *ethnography*, the subject of this book.

The authors of this book, like the anthropologist described above, conducted (and continue to do) ethnographic research as part of their professional training and careers. All three of us have learned to see the world from the viewpoint of people with cultures different from our own. Significantly, all of us have found our ethnographic experience to be personally transforming and immensely useful, and as we began to teach undergraduate students, we became convinced that the perspective of cultural anthropology is best learned through ethnographic field-work and that undergraduate students are fully capable of doing this kind of research.

This book, now in its second edition and informed by experience gained from guiding over 6,000 undergraduate students through ethnographic field research over 33 years, is the result. It is designed to help undergraduates share in this cultural experience, once limited to graduate students and professional anthropologists, by detailing a way to do shorter, but significant, ethnographic studies in the context of North American society. It describes an ethnographic technique, ***ethnosemantics***, which is based on interviewing, and discusses strategies for setting up and carrying out an ethnographic field study.

To help you produce a successful ethnography, the pages that follow are organized around several important questions. What is culture? What is ethnographic research and how does it differ from other social research strategies? What is *a* culture and how can you identify one inside a complex society? How do you set up an ethnographic study, choose a microculture, and find and approach an informant? How do you explain your research to cultural informants and obtain their informed consent? What are your ethical responsibilities during the ethnographic process? What are ethnographic questions and how do you ask them and why? How do you record your data? How do you organize and analyze what you have learned? How do you write an ethnography? What good is ethnographic research and how is it used in the world of work? What are some examples of student ethnographies? To get started, let's look first at the concept of culture, since the discovery and description of culture are the objects of ethnography.

Culture

What Is Culture?

It is hard to avoid the term *culture* these days. (Interestingly, the public rarely used the term when the first edition of this book was published in 1972 and only started to do so in popular discourse within the past 25 years.) For example, we talk about "corporate culture." We hear that continents are rich in culture. We have offices of "multicultural affairs" and we participate in cultural sensitivity programs. We are told that a particular social disagreement is caused by a cultural problem. Although we are pleased that the concept has made it into the everyday thinking of the general public, it is important for beginning ethnographers to understand how *anthropologists,* who first invented the term, use it today.

Culture was first defined by British anthropologist E. B. Tylor in 1871. He wrote:

> Culture or civilization, taken in its wide ethnographic sense, is that complex whole which includes knowledge, belief, art, morals, law, custom, and any other capabilities and habits acquired by man as a member of society. (1871:1)

Tylor, as well as other social thinkers of his day, was impressed by accounts of strikingly different human groups living in other parts of the world. These reports were usually sent back to Europe by missionaries, travelers, and colonial officials, and Tylor often asked them to do fieldwork for him. Tylor used the term culture to name the system of knowledge, behavior, and material goods associated with such groups. In essence, he argued that groups of people were different and unique because they created different learned and shared ways of life. Tylor's characterization of culture is often called the *omnibus definition*, because he included in it everything he could think of (except biological ancestry) that might distinguish a group.

Because it best fits the kind of research we describe in this book, we use a more focused definition of culture. We define **culture** as: *knowledge that is learned and shared and that people use to generate behavior and interpret experience.*

This definition has consequences for research because you can't actually see knowledge; it is located in people's heads. As a result, a group's culture has to be inferred from its members' behavior and objects people have produced. We call these two sources of evidence, *cultural behavior* and *cultural artifacts.* The method used in this book seeks largely to deduce cultural knowledge from people's speech (a kind of behavior), so it emphasizes interviewing.

Attributes of Culture

Culture is a kind of knowledge, but we need to distinguish it from at least one other kind of knowledge, *personal knowledge*. To separate cultural knowledge from personal knowledge we need to identify its key attributes.

Culture Is Learned.   The first attribute has to do with how we acquire cultural knowledge. Culture is *learned*, not biologically inherited. Children learn their culture from their parents and group members. They imitate what they see going on around them and are often corrected by others when they make mistakes. The same goes for adults when they find themselves part of a new group or unfamiliar situation. For example, when you first arrived at your college or university, you probably had no idea what the buildings were named, where they were located, or what their functions were. This information is part of inside college culture and is usually unknown to outsiders. Although second nature to college community participants, this inside knowledge must be learned by new members if they are to become part of the group.

The idea that culture is learned knowledge counteracts the notion that members of groups (think of race here) biologically inherit shared behavior. Anthropologists reject this notion. They argue that groups are organized and their members act according to knowledge they have learned.

Culture Is Shared.   A second attribute of culture distinguishes it from personal knowledge. Culture is *shared*; it is social knowledge, not knowledge unique to an individual. This becomes painfully apparent when you try to join a group of people who are speaking a foreign, and to you, unintelligible, language. The members of the group seem to understand one another. They should, since they *share* the part of culture, language, that produces the speech sounds and symbolic meanings.

The distinction between shared and unshared (personal) knowledge is not as neat as it seems, however. We believe personal knowledge is mentally organized in a way similar to cultural knowledge; it simply is not shared with other group members. For example, one of the authors once owned a 1964 Volkswagen microbus. Its brand and model name are culturally shared categories as are many of its attributes—lack of engine power, instability in a crosswind, opposed four-cylinder engine, constant need of valve adjustment. But for its owner, it had several attributes that gave it meaning that only he knew (or cared) about—the time it ran out of gas rolling down a hill into Kansas City and the little oil leak behind number-four cylinder, for example. In this sense, all the categories that make up cultural knowledge probably have a dimension of personal meaning, but it's the shared meaning that ethnographers seek to discover.

A constant problem for ethnographers is the need to separate informants' personal knowledge (and their opinions) from their cultural knowledge. In short, the study of culture tells us something about how *groups* are organized and why one group can be distinguished from another. The study of personal knowledge will tell about an *individual's* characteristics and why one person behaves differently from another within a cultural group.

Culture Generates Behavior. In the past, many anthropologists defined culture as a kind of behavior or at least a system of behavioral patterns. Here we treat behavior as an outcome of culture. We argue that people use their cultural knowledge to *generate behavior*. For example, most people in the United States greet each other by shaking hands, saying "Hi," or both. Depending on which region of the country we are from, what ethnic group we belong to, and our relationship to the person we meet, we might hug, kiss, or use a series of phrases such as, "How are you?" or "What's up?" In rural Rajasthan, India, people also greet one another, but they use a different system of cultural knowledge to generate the greeting behavior. They may put their palms together and say "*Ram, Ram ji.*" Or they may clasp each other's hands using the same prayer-like hand position and say the same phrase or just intone a nonword, "*vah,*" two or three times. Their culture also defines three other ways to greet depending on the formality of the situation.

We are not arguing here that cultural knowledge regularly requires people to act in only one way, although that may be true in a few situations. Instead we are saying that culture defines a range of behavioral possibilities from which people can choose. Take dress for example. A look at most crowds of people in the United States and Canada reveals a variety of clothing styles and colors. But the culture sets limits. It's against the cultural rules for students to attend class naked, for example, a behavior that would be the normal, culturally approved "dress" for some groups of Amazonian Indians. One way to think about this is to view culture as a road map. If you want to drive to a particular location there are usually a large number of ways to get there. The map permits variety. But it also limits your options since you can't drive through buildings, forests, or other barriers.

Culture Interprets Experience. A fourth attribute of culture is that people *use culture to interpret experience*. If an instructor walked into one of your classes wearing a scuba diving suit complete with flippers, you would most likely be startled if not amazed because our culture says instructors don't dress that way for class. (This does not mean that people don't do "off the wall" things occasionally. It simply means that we judge such actions as culturally inappropriate, as outside the rules.) When we enter any kind of social situation, we use our cultural knowledge to identify where we are and what is going on so that we will know how to behave.

Kinds of Culture

Finally, we believe there are two kinds of culture to be concerned about when we do ethnographic research: tacit culture and explicit culture.

Tacit culture is the cultural knowledge people don't put into words. The classic example of tacit culture used by many anthropologists when they teach the concept is speaking distance. Years ago anthropologist Edward T. Hall (1959) noted that North Americans observed four kinds of speaking distances—intimate, personal, social, and public—without knowing it. Although Hall gave them names, North Americans have no words for these distances. Your parents never admonished you to "use the personal speaking distance" when you were growing up.

Language, itself, also serves as an excellent example of tacit culture. We keep utterances apart by using what linguists call phonemes (the minimal speech sounds such as /t/ and /e/ that keep utterances apart). There are cultural rules about the order in which phonemes can appear. One is that we never use the sound /ng/ to begin a word in English. This rule is tacit. We don't have a word for this arrangement nor are we conscious of it. Speaking distances and rules for arranging phonemes are tacit cultural categories and can only be inferred by watching and listening to people.

Explicit culture consists of cultural categories that are coded in language. We speak of "cars," "presidents," "toenails," and any number of things, real or imagined, using words. Indeed, much of culture is explicit and coded in language.

We emphasize the distinction between tacit culture and explicit culture here because it highlights different research approaches for ethnographers. Since they are not named, tacit cultural categories must be inferred from observation. Hall didn't ask people about their speaking distances, they had no words for what they were doing. He and his students patiently observed interaction between North Americans to infer what the tacit cultural distance rules are.

People can talk about explicit culture so interviewing or simply listening to them speak is an important way to discover their cultural knowledge. Consequently, the interviewing method presented in this book is best suited for the discovery of explicit culture. (Note that anthropologists often do both observation and interviewing simultaneously. Participant observation is a hallmark of ethnographic research, but time consuming and usually less structured.)

Ethnography

What Is Ethnography?

The goal of this book is to introduce you to ethnographic fieldwork. We define *ethnography* as the process of discovering and describing a culture. As we noted above, culture is the knowledge a group of people uses to generate behavior and interpret experience. Ethnography is the formal research approach used to acquire the cultural knowledge of a social group. It also includes the description, often written but sometimes visually or orally presented, used to convey information about the group's culture to a larger audience.

Although this book presents a systematic way to do ethnography, all of us, without knowing it, engage informally in a kind of ethnographic process every day. As soon as we are born, we begin to acquire culture much as anthropologists do. We learn a culturally generated language by listening to people talk and trying to speak ourselves. By watching, listening, and asking questions we learn the cultural rules for how to dress and thousands of details about how to behave. We learn to expect people to behave in certain ways and what their motivations to act are likely to be. As we grow older and encounter different groups, we must learn the cultural knowledge that organizes these smaller social entities. The process of learning culture never really stops, since culture changes rapidly along with our association with new and different people and groups. Our aim as anthropologists is to make this informal ethnography into a more conscious, highly structured, and efficient process.

Naive Realism

We have argued that culture is the system of knowledge that structures our day-to-day world. But the fact that we personally live by a culture we have learned and internalized presents a problem when we try to do ethnographic research. Culture causes us to see the world in a particular way, one we come to believe is real. Blue is a color, we think. So is green. These are real colors for most of us living in North America. An avocado is a vegetable. The letter "d" is a sound. Our culture gives us an endless list of ways to see the world and we learn to believe that these categories reflect the *real* nature of the world.

Anthropologists call this cultural perspective, *naive realism*, the unconscious belief that the way we culturally see the world is actually the way it is. But members of other cultural groups, who have learned another culture, often see the same world in a different way. For example, Bhil tribal people living in central India name the colors we call blue and green by a single term. For them it is one color, not two. They are just as sure that their category reflects the real world as we are about ours. In Latin America, avocados are a fruit, not a vegetable. Hindi speakers in India have four sound categories, /d/, /dh/, /D/, and /Dh/ where we have only /d/. These are distinct sounds for them but we can hardly hear the difference.

Naive realism often inhibits the ethnographic process since if you think you already know how the world really is it is easy to unconsciously *assume* that other people, even if they seem foreign, see it the same way. Because of this, it is easy to miss cultural differences and to use your own cultural perspective to interpret the actions of others.

Ethnocentrism

Ethnocentrism also gets in the way of learning someone else's culture. Ethnocentrism is defined as the belief and feeling that one's culture is best. It causes us to judge the actions of culturally different people. When Bhil mothers are shocked to learn that American infants and children sleep by themselves, not in the same bed as their parents or siblings, which is the rule in their culture, they are being ethnocentric. So are Americans when they are horrified by the way Indian villagers throw rocks at and kick their dogs. Ethnocentrism makes us judge other people's cultural knowledge, and inhibits our ability to learn it.

To manage ethnocentrism, it is important for anthropologists to be consciously aware of their assumptions and biases during the ethnographic process. Awareness means that ethnographers try to control for their naive realism and ethnocentrism and see other people's cultures as different but reasonable systems of knowledge.

Subjects, Respondents, and Informants

To understand the nature of ethnographic research better, it is helpful to compare it to other forms of research on human beings. One way to do this is to look at what researchers call the people they study. Psychologists usually refer to those they study as *subjects*. (The term is now also used more broadly as in "human subjects research.") The term stems from a kind of psychological behaviorist research where individuals are "subjects" of experiments. The goal of behaviorist research is not to discover what people consciously think they are doing, but to see how people will behave under certain conditions. Researchers use *detached observation* to collect data (observation of subject's behavior through one-way mirrors is a common technique). Such research is usually theory driven in the sense that the experiments are designed to test a theory. Observed behaviors are categorized by the observer, not the subjects.

Sociologists (also political scientists and others) traditionally call the people they study *respondents*. The term reflects a common sociological method, **survey research**, in which large numbers of people are asked the same series of questions on a questionnaire and "respond" by choosing among a limited number of answers. Survey research is often associated with theory testing although it is also used to discover individual preferences and opinions. Survey researchers assume they know the culture and language of their respondents and use surveys to generate statistical data that confirm or disconfirm hypotheses. Most people you approach for an interview in the United States will expect you to ask them survey-style questions, a problem we will discuss later.

Anthropologists call the people they study **informants** because they inform us about their cultural knowledge. The term has more recently become a problem because it resembles the word "informer," someone who is a snitch, or someone who shares information, and in so doing causes harm to others. Since many anthropologists continue to use the term informant, we carry on that convention here for lack of a better alternative. (Cultural informants is the topic of chapter 3.)

Instead of starting with a theory to test, anthropologists usually seek to *discover* their informants' views of what they are doing. The challenge for ethnographers is to help their informants remember and express their cultural knowledge. The goal is to encourage informants to teach anthropologists their culture. That is why we said earlier in this chapter that the method described in this book is discovery oriented. Because of this, you don't need to know anthropological theory or choose a social problem in order to guide your ethnographic fieldwork.

In short, the kind of ethnography we suggest you do here seeks to find out what other people know. It does not ask you to classify a subject's behavior based on observation or test theories by asking hundreds of people the same set of directed questions. Think of the ethnographic process like this: Informants are our teachers; we are their students. We are trying to learn how to view the world the way they do. We hope to learn the "inside information" that guides their actions and conveys meaning. To do this we need a field method to help them teach us systematically without imposing our views and interests on what they tell us. Learning their culture and later writing about it is our ethnographic goal.

2

Microcultures

In the last chapter we defined culture as knowledge shared by a social group. We noted that ethnography was the research approach used by anthropologists to discover cultural knowledge and produce an ethnographic account with the help of group members. In this chapter we will discuss how to identify individual cultures and choose one that will be both convenient and easy to study.

What Are Microcultures?

In the early days of anthropology, identifying a particular culture to study seemed easy. Most groups were named (although the names were often given to them by outsiders) and thought to be culturally distinct. Many groups lived in discernable territories. When anthropologists proposed to do an ethnographic study, they normally identified a named group they sought to learn about, traveled to the area where it was located, found a community willing to put up with them, settled in, and began to learn the culture. By the time they left the field one or two years later, they had information about the whole way of life of the people. When they wrote the ethnographies (descriptive books) that resulted from their research, they tended to ascribe the people's cultural knowledge they had discovered to the group as a whole. As a result, it is usual to see anthropologists writing about such groups as the Yanomamo, Burmese,

Tikopia, and Santal. The authors of this book, for example, have published accounts of the Kwakiutl, Bhils, and Nuer, among others.

You face a different set of challenges as you prepare to conduct a study in complex North American society. You can't really choose to interview just anyone who was born and brought up there. The U.S. and Canadian national culture is so broad and society so complex, that the task would be impossible given the short time you have to do the study.

In the 1800s and first half of the 1900s, anthropologists pursued research in North American Indian societies. Later, when a few anthropologists first tried to do research on other groups within U.S. society, they usually chose cultures belonging to ethnic groups, people who had immigrated to the United States but still maintained some of their original culture. Although this option reduces the scope of study within the researcher's native country (the United States in this example), it still requires major time commitments, possible language learning, coping with identity politics, and other challenges and complications. We advise our students not to do this kind of study for these and several other reasons.

This leaves a third option: the study of still smaller groups that exist inside society. We call such groups and their cultural knowledge *microcultures*. To understand what we mean by this classification and later, how to spot one, it is useful to place the term in a set of three kinds of cultures based on size and scope. For purposes of the research described here, we reserve the noun *culture* to refer to national cultures, such as U.S. culture or French culture, or to culturally distinctive groups that are politically independent or at least are not well integrated into a larger society. Such cultures define a whole way of life for their members and are consequently large and complex.

We use the term *subculture* to refer to a whole way of life culture found within a larger society. (Note that many social scientists use the term subculture to refer to any culture found inside a national culture. We are defining a third-level kind of cultural group here.) Often such groups are ethnic groups made up of people from other parts of the world. Their cultures may have been autonomous at one time but now define people's lives within the group as it exists inside the national group. The Nuer who have emigrated from Africa to the United States still maintain a subculture. So, in the past, did German, Italian, Finnish, and a host of other immigrants to the U.S. A nonethnic group that can be called a subculture are the tramps studied by one of the authors (Spradley 1970). Although not an ethnic group, tramps have created a large and complex culture that guides their lives 24 hours a day inside U.S. culture.

In this book, we focus on microcultures. Microcultures are similar to subcultures in that they exist inside larger, complex societies. They differ in one major respect, however: they do not define a whole way of life.

They are the cultures associated with groups that form for a variety of reasons but do not consume every hour of their members' time. All of us participate in several microcultures at any time in our lives. All of us must learn the cultural knowledge specific to such groups when we interact with other members belonging to them.

If, for example, you are a server at a local restaurant, you will discover that there is a server culture there. It is a good example of a microculture. So is almost any occupational group. Recreational groups—sports teams, motorcycle clubs, gaming societies—are also examples of microcultures. Church groups are microcultures. Residential groups such as families, and dormitory and nursing home residents, often display an inside culture.

To complicate matters, microcultures can be found inside microcultures. For example, take a bank. There is a bank culture that everyone who works there shares. They know what the jobs in the bank are called. They know about the times for working, eating, and taking breaks. They have a common sense of how to dress. Before the advent of automatic deposits, everyone in the bank knew about such events as "social security day" when retirees lined up to deposit or cash their government checks. But there are groups of bank employees who form subgroups with their own microcultures. There is *teller culture*, for example. It is somewhat different from *guard culture* and *personal banker culture*. This is because each employee group has its own goals, requirements, and problems. Tellers, for example, share special inside knowledge about how to handle particular managers or what to do when their accounts don't balance at the end of the day. They may share ways to stretch breaks or find time to eat on busy days.

All of us are surrounded by microcultures. We change our participation from one to another as we interact during the day. For example, if you live in a dorm at your college or university, you may get up in the morning and participate in *floor culture* (or even *roommate culture*). If a parent visits you, you may switch to *family culture*. If you play on the soccer team in the afternoon, you begin to use *soccer team culture*.

But what about the cultural knowledge shared by microcultural group members that is also shared with the national or at least a wider microculture? If you are brought up in the United States, much of your interaction will be guided by national culture. Doesn't this make it difficult to identify a boundary that marks off one microculture from another?

It is true that whether or not you are talking to a parent, dormitory mate, or fellow soccer player, you most likely speak English, which is part of your national culture. Your speaking distances and many other ways to interact will also be generated by the larger culture. But there is still a unique microculture that characterizes these groups. When we study microcultures, we concentrate on the "inside" culture of the group, not its national content. Stockbrokers, for example, talk about "the cage," "bull pen," "red herrings," and "puts," not things most Americans know about. In addition, some cultural knowledge that looks national or regional often turns out to have inside meaning. The term *group*, for example, has a general meaning for most North Americans but a special meaning for members of a twelve-step program like Alcoholics Anonymous. The category, "rain," has a usual, shared meaning for everyone, but a special meaning for members of the Gold Wing Road Riders Association, a motorcycle club whose members often ride in such weather.

Studies of everyday microcultures may seem trivial at first but they are not. Many of the conflicts and inefficiencies that plague government agencies and private corporations occur because of cross-cultural misunderstandings between members of different microcultures within such groups. More and more professional anthropologists are hired to conduct ethnographies inside companies to solve just such problems. (See chapter 9 for some specific examples of using ethnography in this way.)

Locating and Choosing a Microculture

The first task you face as you prepare to do an ethnography is to choose a microculture, although some student ethnographers find it useful to find a cultural informant first, then choose a microculture that person is part of as the object of study. We suggest you make your choice by following a couple of steps.

First, *make a list of every microculture you think you could study.* Our students have gone about this task in a number of ways. Most list microcultures that interest them. (It is a good idea to start with a number of possibilities to provide backups, because you don't always have control over whether a particular idea will work.) There are several ways you can look for possible microcultures to put on your list. You can look in the yellow pages of the phone book for likely businesses and other organizations that have microcultures. You might walk through neighborhoods near your school, looking for likely settings where microcultures might be found. You can ask friends what kind of groups they are part of that might be suitable to study. We have even had students who looked on the Internet for chat groups to study or called friends in other cities to ask them about their participation in microcultures with the idea of interviewing them over the phone. Below are some ideas for a list of microcultures:

firefighter	nursing home attendant
tattooist	coin collector
motorcycle club member	flight attendant

skateboarder	personal trainer
research team member	tae kwan do student
college custodian	health food store worker
stockbroker	fraternity member
rock climber	fourth grader
social worker	bank teller
daycare worker	football team member
fashion model	dog breeder
aerobics instructor	bar bouncer
dairy farmer	beautician
bird watcher	fast-food counter person
hardware store clerk	barrel racer
restaurant server	band member
mortician	floor nurse
emergency room doctor	massage therapist
radio announcer	landscape architect
bus driver	car sales representative
high school teacher	taxi dispatcher

Next, *choose a microculture from the list that will be easy to study.* We believe that anthropologists can learn from informants belonging to almost any microculture. Since this will probably be your first ethnographic research experience, we also believe it is best to choose microcultures that are easiest to study. Remember that the goal of this first ethnographic excursion is not only to discover the nature of an interesting microculture, but to learn how to *do* ethnographic research well so you can use it in the future. If you choose a difficult microculture, problems can easily sabotage this learning process.

A few rules have emerged from the experience of students over the years that may help you choose a microculture that will be easier to learn about. Remember, however, that no microculture will qualify under every rule. A structured microculture may not be in current operation. A social microculture may be in the process of change. The final choice of a microculture requires you to assess it against the criteria with the hope that the choice is more, rather than less, beneficial for study. And to repeat, always have some backups ready in case your first choice falls through.

Now let's look at the list of rules for what makes a microculture easier to study.

- Choose small microcultures, not large ones. It is easier to manage a small microculture in detail than a large one on the surface. For example, it is easier to study the dining hall eating culture at your college or university than the culture of the whole institution.

- Choose structured microcultures marked by regularity and routine, not microcultures marked by variety and unpredictability. It is better to study the microculture of an assembly-line worker than the culture of a community organizer (where the latter never seems to do the same thing twice).

- Choose social microcultures, not individualistic ones. It is easier to study the culture of flight attendants than it is of beekeepers. It is usually more interesting too.

- Choose an accessible microculture, not one that takes three hours to get to. Your time and your informants' availability are variables to consider when you choose a microculture.

- Choose old and stable microcultures, not new and changing ones. It is easier to investigate the routine of tellers in a bank where things have been the same for years than it is to study tellers in a newly opened bank where the culture is still forming.

- Choose current microcultures, not defunct ones. It is better to study server culture in a restaurant that still exists than server culture in a restaurant that no longer is in operation. This way, you can actually visit the cultural setting and your informants can observe and correct information. However, many students have found they can do a kind of cultural oral history successfully on microcultures that no longer exist, so this rule is probably broken more than any other.

- Choose microcultures marked by explicit culture, not ones characterized by tacit culture. It is better to study nursing home attendant culture, which is mostly coded in language and thus explicit, than it is to investigate the culture of an artist or jazz musician where categories and meanings are learned by doing but difficult to talk about.

- Choose open cultures, not closed ones. Any culture designed to hide information from a public is difficult to study. For example, studying "up" in an organization can be more difficult than studying down because people in authority have more to lose if they reveal their inside cultural meanings and strategies. Thus it is more difficult to study bank president culture because bank presidents must manage other people and have the most to lose if they tell about it. Bank tellers, on the other hand, are easier to study because they have less to lose. It is more difficult to study mortician culture, which is designed to hide the grim facts of death, than it is to learn railroad switching culture, which is organized to switch railroad cars.

- Choose nonideological cultures, not ones with strong beliefs. It is more difficult to study microcultures that have a mission to teach an ideology such as religions, ethnic identity groups, and political movements. Informants tend to give you an ideal version of their culture rather than the day-to-day information you must know if you are to discover how to act appropriately in the group.

- Choose nontranslational cultures, not ones designed to manage impressions. It is more difficult to study cultures that are designed to relate to a public (teachers, priests, and public relations people) than it is to study ones without such missions. Informants will seek to control the impression they give you just as they do for the public.

- Choose microcultures whose folk language is English, not cultures encoded in some other language. It is better to study almost any English-speaking microculture than one coded in another language. If you speak another language and choose a microculture whose members also routinely speak it, your field notes will have to be transcribed in that language and your paper will have the added task of translating concepts into English. Note that anthropologists do this all the time but we believe it is better to avoid this complication when you first start ethnographic training.

- Choose unfamiliar microcultures, not familiar ones. A problem with ethnographic research in your own society is the tendency to miss interesting differences and contrasts because you are so used to what goes on around you. Anthropologists working in very different societies find it much easier to see differences and remain naive, because the culture they seek to learn is so different. A problem you will face from the start is to maintain naiveté, to imagine you are a stranger to the world and that you must ask basic questions about everything. It is easier to do this if you choose a microculture that you know nothing about.

- Choose microcultures outside your own social world, not ones in it. It is better to study the culture of a sewing shop owner than it is the culture of your college financial aid director. The latter individual must deal with you personally, thus may hide the strategies for doing so. It is tempting to evade this rule. For example, if you have a work-study job or are a volunteer working with a neighborhood group, you are already in a different microculture and it is tempting to interview coworkers about it. But since you also have a role (social identity) inside the group, members are likely to wonder why you are asking basic questions about their behavior when you already should know about them.

- Avoid dangerous and illegal microcultures. Although they may look exciting and exotic, illegal microcultures—drug dealers, pimps, theft rings—should be avoided. (We declare illegal microcultures off limits to our students.) Members of illegal scenes are naturally suspicious of the motives of anyone looking into their affairs and can pose a real danger to ethnographers. Authorities can try to force you to testify against your informants if the latter are arrested and brought to trial. Protecting cultural informants is an essential part of an ethnographer's ethical responsibility.

When you choose a microculture, we think it is a good idea to evaluate it against this list. (We have our students write and present such an evaluation in class.) That way you can prepare yourself for disadvantages you might face and think about ways to deal with them.

As we noted at the beginning of this section, no microculture meets all these requirements. Furthermore, many students have managed to overcome microcultural liabilities by choosing the right informants or in some other way inventing ways around them. Ethnographic research is a personal business, and although we stress rules for doing this kind of research here, we recognize the need to break them will often occur. But we urge you to try to follow the steps we have outlined here as you choose a microculture. Once you do so, the next step is to find one or a few people from the scene to become your cultural informants.

Cultural Informants

Choosing a microculture is only the first step in setting up an ethnographic study. The second step, and one that is often more difficult and anxiety producing, is to find one or a small number of cultural informants who are willing to teach you their microculture. Working with informants is the hallmark of ethnographic fieldwork and involves an ongoing personal relationship. This is often not true for social scientists who use other forms of research. They may never lay eyes on questionnaire respondents, never meet people they observe, or at best, interview respondents only once face-to-face or over the phone. Anthropologists, on the other hand, usually spend long hours with their cultural informants, often becoming their friends and in some cases, part of their communities. Indeed, many of us were attracted to the discipline because of the "humanness" that characterizes ethnographic research and writing.

Most anthropologists, including almost all of our students when they begin an ethnographic research project, find locating willing cultural informants to be a challenging and anxiety producing process. The best way to think about this is to imagine what it would be like if a stranger came up to you at work and asked you "out of the blue" if you would be willing to be interviewed for a study about what you do there. Immediately, you would wonder who this person is. What kind of study is it? What does he or she want to know? What will the information you relate be used for? Is there a hidden agenda to all of this? Your suspicions would be natural under any circumstance but probably intensified in North America because almost everyone here has been bombarded by phone calls from telemarketers and ceaseless and often disingenuous advertising on television, radio, and the Internet. Furthermore, like most North Americans, you are probably busy and likely to protect your time and privacy.

The challenge associated with this initial contact is what you will face as you seek to locate informants and begin your ethnographic study. Happily, most anthropologists and anthropology students manage this trial well, but they also discover that once an ethnographer/cultural informant relationship is established, some degree of tension will always remain as researchers strive to develop and maintain rapport with their informants.

In this chapter we will look at ways to locate cultural informants, attributes of a good informant, strategies to allay informant distrust, ways to introduce yourself and explain the ethnographic project, and the initial steps necessary to meet your ethical obligations.

Locating Cultural Informants

Finding potential informants can be as easy as approaching someone you already know who is part of the microculture you wish to study, or as difficult as searching the yellow pages and the Internet or making "cold calls" to strangers in hopes of finding links to a microculture that might yield names of people you could interview. Let's start with the easiest approach.

Find an Informant You Already Know

The simplest way to locate an informant is to use a strategy for choosing a microculture described in the last chapter: talk to someone you know who is a member of an interesting microculture. In essence, by contacting an acquaintance about a microculture, you automatically identify a cultural informant. One student ethnographer, for example, asked each of her friends about the groups they participated in. One noted that she had been working part-time for three years as a nursing assistant at a local retirement home. This sounded interesting to the student and she immediately recruited her friend to be her cultural informant. This approach solves not only the challenges of finding a microculture and an informant, it eases the problem of generating initial rapport and trust with the informant. There are drawbacks to this approach, however. You will be limited to studying only the microcultures your acquaintances participate in and you will forgo a typical ethnographic experience, entering a cultural setting as a total stranger. Also, when your informants are your friends, it is sometimes difficult to change your roles as friends to the roles of ethnographer and cultural informant. As we will see later, ethnographic interviewing is not like day-to-day friendly conversation, and this may be difficult for a friend to accept or play along with.

Find an Informant "Cold Turkey"

You may elect to choose a microculture first, then make a direct approach to a stranger who could act as an informant. For example, Jennifer Boehlke, whose paper appears in this book, recruited an informant by visiting a tattoo shop and asking if anyone would be willing to be interviewed by her. After some hesitation, a tattooist agreed to serve in that role. Alex Rubenstein, whose paper also appears later in this book, followed much the same procedure. He walked into a local firehouse and simply asked if someone there would be willing to serve as an informant. Another student made contact with a skateboarder by hanging out at a plaza where young aficionados of the microculture practiced their sport. Even then, it took him three visits before he could successfully interact with the skateboarders and recruit a willing informant.

The direct approach may have to take place over the phone, either because the microculture has a formal location, such as a business office or school building, or because it is impractical or off limits to visit. One student, for example, wished to interview a production line worker at a local car assembly plant. He could not visit the production line at the plant in person because of company policy, so he called the workers' union and received some names of likely informants. After his fourth or fifth call, a man agreed to meet him and later became his informant.

The direct approach gives you the chance to experience what it is like to enter the field as a stranger, but it also is the most difficult to do; it can lead to many rejections, take the most time (time may be crucial when your study must fit into a quarter or semester), and cause you the most anxiety since it is stressful to approach total strangers. When using the cold-call approach, it is especially prudent to keep your options open and have a backup microculture in mind if your first try proves unfeasible.

Find an Informant through a Go-Between

A third way to locate an informant is through the intercession of a go-between, a person you know but who also is acquainted with a suitable informant. Take the experience of one of our students, for example. She wished to learn about the culture of the fourth graders who attended a nearby grammar school, but she did not know any members of the class. She also hesitated to visit the school and ask permission to enter the classroom to find an informant that way because she had heard that many schools are unwilling to give approval to research enterprises that are beyond their control. So she began to ask student friends if they knew of any fourth graders living nearby. None did, so she began to query faculty members. Luckily, a professor had a child in fourth grade and once the student described the project to the parents, they gave her permission to do the ethnography, although they asked that interviews take place at their house, not at the school. You can also widen your search by asking go-betweens to suggest other people who could act as go-betweens and who might know someone from a particular microculture.

The help of go-betweens has one advantage: Because go-betweens are often known to both the researchers and their prospective informants, there is an initial degree of trust that increases an informant's feelings of security. This often enhances their willingness to become informants.

Sometimes friends you initially asked to serve as informants may decline but be willing to act as go-betweens. This is what happened to Melissa Cowell (her paper also appears later in this volume) when she discovered that a high school friend had been working as an exotic dancer. The friend at first agreed to be Melissa's informant, but after preliminary interviews felt embarrassed and recruited a coworker to take her place. The change turned out to be an advantage in another way; the second informant, perhaps because she didn't know Melissa personally, felt freer to talk more openly about her sensitive occupation.

Go-betweens can pose problems, however. For example, a go-between may outrank an informant in the microculture they share. Teachers outrank their students. Factory shift managers outrank their assembly line workers. Such go-betweens may censor what informants say or inhibit their responses in other ways.

For example, one of our students asked the principal of a parochial grammar school to act as a go-between, and the principal named a suitable third-grade informant and set up a meeting between the student and the little girl. When the ethnographer arrived to do her first interview, she was ushered into an empty room. Soon a small girl wearing her school uniform stepped through the door, accompanied by a nun who introduced herself as Sister Mary, and both sat down across from the researcher. After explaining the project and asking her first question, the ethnographer soon discovered that Sister Mary's presence inhibited the third grader from being completely open. Soon, Sister Mary was asking questions of the little girl herself, many of them aimed at producing responses that would place the school in a positive light. In addition, the student ethnographer began to suspect that the third grader had been chosen for her "reliability," and the presence of the nun prevented any possibility of learning an inside view of third-grade culture. In short, it is best to avoid this situation by using go-betweens who are not part of a microculture or whose status is the same or lower than your informant's.

Attributes of a Good Informant

Finding a suitable go-between is important, but choosing good informants is even more vital, remembering that this is your first ethnographic research experience and you will learn more about the method if things go smoothly. Several attributes of good cultural informants emerge from the experience of our students. Let us look at the most important ones.

- A cultural informant should know the culture well, not be just learning it. It is better to choose seniors as informants about student culture at your college or university than newly arrived first-year students. The latter will have difficulty thinking of cultural categories and rules because they have not learned them yet.

- An informant should be currently involved in the culture, not previously involved. Culture becomes so routine and unconscious that informants who are no longer involved have difficulty remembering the special knowledge they previously used to generate behavior and interpret experience within a group. Current involvement makes it possible for the informant to recall information more easily and observe what goes on in the scenes associated with their microculture. Their information will be fresher and they will find it easier to remember details if they are actually "doing" the scene. We should point out that in some cases, it is quite possible to help informants recall information about the past in some detail. For example, some students have found informants whose microcultures were not currently in operation, such as summer camp counselors or being a senior at a boarding school and were able to ask questions that facilitated detailed answers.

- Someone who is verbal and social makes a better informant than someone who is a loner or who dislikes talking. Since you will want detail in your study, someone who fills in facts automatically without constant probing and who tells stories easily will be more valuable, to say nothing about more fun, to interview. The case of a student ethnographer who interviewed a worker at a local library comes to mind. The informant hated his job and seemed to dislike social interaction. When asked a basic ethnographic question, such as "Could you describe your average day at the library?" he responded, "There is not much to tell. I come to work, do stuff in the stacks, and go home." As interviewing continued over the semester-long study, the student ethnographer described the experience as "like pulling teeth" and "prying words loose." It was not only difficult for the researcher to learn much about the informant's microculture, it was hard for her to maintain her own enthusiasm about the study.

On the other hand, it is possible to choose an informant who is too verbal. The first interview or two may go fine, but later interviews may be difficult to control, and some degree of control is necessary to successful ethnographic interviewing.

- An informant should be located nearby and have time for the research rather than live far away or be too busy to get together for interviews. An informant located 20 miles away may require a lot of travel time. Doctors and many businesspeople often lack time for interviews and either fail to agree to do a study at all or balk at continuing the interviews once they figure out how much time they will actually take. In addition, as the paper on midwife culture by Natasha Winegar illustrates, you may have to gauge how much flexibility you have to accommodate an informant who doesn't have control over his or her schedule and availability.

One Informant or Many?

We recommend that you limit semester-long (or shorter) ethnographic studies to a single informant or, at most, two or three informants. You will find it necessary to build trust and a comfortable relationship with your cultural informant, and this requires time. And given the kinds of questions we suggest you ask as you interview, each new informant requires the same kind of "development" time, and time is something you won't have much of.

Many of our students question this advice. Doesn't interviewing just one informant bias the ethnography? How can you be sure that what an informant tells you is shared by other members of the microculture? Doesn't this violate scientific reliability?

These are valid questions and indeed, most anthropologists who conduct longer ethnographic studies interview many cultural informants. But ethnographic research is different from survey research, with its carefully drawn respondent samples, sets of questions asked to all, and use of statistics to interpret results. Although informants constantly give us opinions whether we ask for them or not, ethnography is not opinion research. Instead, it is the discovery of categories that members of a group share and that name and give meaning to the natural and social contexts in which they live. The kind of information anthropologists collect is often basic—how do you brush your teeth? What do you say to be polite? What ways are there to dress? What strategies are there to avoid a speeding ticket? None of us learns our culture (and microcultures) by constructing a questionnaire. Instead, we learn it by observing and asking questions just as anthropologists do.

Determining how much and how widely cultural information is shared is a problem, however. As we will note later, we suggest you ask questions that refer to the group—"Could you describe the average day for police officers here at the station?" instead of, "Could you describe *your* average day here at the station?" Although you will meet critics of the ethnographic method, the approach is validated by the large number of anthropologists who work as ethnographers in government and private corporations.

Identifying Yourself and Explaining the Project

Once you have found a likely informant, you still must identify yourself, describe your research agenda, and ask that person to participate in the study. We impose a hard and fast rule on our students about identifying themselves. They must reveal that they are anthropology students in a particular class and that they are trying to learn how to discover a group's microculture. Under no circumstances do we permit them to misrepresent themselves.

The identity, *anthropologist*, has initial pitfalls that you may have to overcome. Most people have no idea what cultural anthropology is. Most identify the discipline with paleontology and archaeology. Second, they don't know what ethnography is. They expect that you will ask them a battery of questions from a survey protocol. They suspect that you have in mind a social problem or point of view that guides your research. The idea that you are just trying to discover what one needs to know to act and understand things in their microcultural terms seems foreign, and sometimes trivial, to them. And when you tell them that you would like to do several hour-long interviews, they may look even more critically at your motivations.

A couple of things will help, though. The fact that you are a student, and many people are used to students asking for help on field projects, will make people feel at ease. To help people understand the type of research you are conducting, use examples to explain what ethnography is. Describe traditional anthropological fieldwork in foreign societies, where an anthropologist often does not know enough about a people to ask directed questions. Instead, you say, anthropologists need to discover the knowledge it takes to *be* the people in that society. Some years ago one of the authors of this book interviewed stockbrokers at a local firm. When at times they seemed confused about what he was doing, he used to say, "This is a foreign culture around here. It's just like Highland New Guinea," and point out that it would be hard for a stranger, unfamiliar with the stockbroker business, to understand what went on in the office.

Controlling Anxiety

Ethnography can be a scary enterprise. You may have to approach total strangers and, almost like a beggar, ask them for help. Since you are just learning how to interview, there is also the uncertainty about what to say next. Especially at first, field research can cause anxiety. Take consolation in the fact that most people and certainly most anthropologists feel anxiety when they enter a strange social setting; it is simply to be expected.

One way to lessen anxiety is to choose an informant you already know. Or, you can interview someone who is younger than you. Children are less threatening for most people so you can choose a microculture where children act as informants. Read and reread applicable sections of this book. The more you know about what you are doing, the more confident you will be. Try doing a practice session where you play the role of an anthropologist approaching an informant for the first time. (You can also do this with a first interview.) Finally, as you progress in your study you can work to establish rapport, the harmonious relationship between two people.

Recording Ethnographic Field Data

As you will learn in the next chapter, the ethnosemantic interview method requires that you record the actual words, called *folk terms*, which members of a microculture use when they talk with each other. You may also observe settings that characterize the microculture. Since it is nearly impossible to remember everything people say or everything you observe, it is important to take notes. We require that our students use tape recorders to record and transcribe their cultural informants' words verbatim. This may seem (and is) a long and tedious process, but it is essential to analysis and to the formulation of future questions. It also provides a detailed and exhaustive record of parts of the informant's culture and minimizes the impact of ethnocentric bias.

We also suggest that students write down some brief notes during interviews, recording *key terms* that might help them ask questions later in the interview or in subsequent interviews. If it seems impossible to record or note down your informant's words during the interview, try to find time as soon after an interview ends as possible to reconstruct what was said and noticed.

Box 3.1   Tape Recorder Tips

Tape recorders can and do malfunction, so it is a good idea to check that your tape recorder is working before you start interviewing. Also, as soon as possible after an interview is finished, make sure you actually recorded the proceedings and that you can hear what was said. If recording failed, as soon as possible write down everything you can remember about the interview. Also, keep a second tape handy along with a full set of extra batteries in case you need them. And don't use the voice recognition feature on your tape recorder if it has one. Keep the recorder on all the time during the interview.

Ethical Responsibilities

Earlier we stated our belief that it is unethical for ethnographers to misrepresent themselves and their research to informants. Here, we want to emphasize another primary ethical principle that should be followed by all anthropologists, the primary duty *not to harm an informant in any way.*

This precept is not as easy to follow as it sounds. We ask our informants to teach us their culture, but in doing so they may tell us things that would somehow harm or embarrass them or members of their microculture if made public. To protect informants, you may have to exclude interesting, even crucial, information from your final ethnographic report. You may also tell informants at the beginning of the study to reveal only cultural information they are comfortable disclosing. Finally, you can ask them to read a draft of your ethnography, checking for sensitive information, and you can change the names of places and people when you write. It is also a good idea to read the Code of Ethics produced by the American Anthropological Association. It can be found on their Web site at http://www.aaanet.org/committees/ethics/ethcode.htm.

Human Subjects Research Requirements

Since the early 1990s, more and more colleges and universities have required researchers who work with human study populations, both students and faculty members, to have their research proposals approved by a Human Subjects Research Committee and to have subjects sign informed consent forms. Both procedures can pose problems for anthropological fieldwork because they were not designed with ethnography in mind. Instead, they emerged as a result of excesses in medical research and other procedures that involved human intervention. A number of notorious cases came to light where experimental subjects were not told what might be done to them nor were researchers themselves fully aware of the consequences of what they were doing to subjects. To insure that such problems would not recur, institutions created safeguards in the form of committees and paperwork.

These measures, however, reflect an experimental research bias and are difficult to apply to ethnographic research. Many institutions have tried to modify review procedures to take social research into consideration, but the discovery-driven participant observation-like nature of ethnography poses a special problem since it is difficult to state a precise research goal or produce a list of detailed research procedures. How, for example, can an informant sign an informed consent form when ethnographers often don't know what questions they will ask until the research is well underway?

Luckily, most anthropologists have been able to work around these problems by explaining the unique requirements of ethnographic research to institutional committees and by struggling as best they can to explain what ethnographic research is like to institutional committees and informants. A helpful document, "AAA statement on Ethnography and Institutional Review Boards," can be accessed at http://www.aaanet.org/stmts/irb.htm.

At our institution, we have organized a research review committee for qualitative research (ethnography is a kind of qualitative research) to look at student research proposals. We have not tried or been required to have informants sign consent forms although we have created one in case it is needed. We have also managed to expedite the review process so ethnographers can get right to work.

We have included copies of two forms below to illustrate what a review and consent process might consist of. The first is a form that student researchers submit to the review committee, which identifies and assesses the microculture and informant they have chosen (see figure 3.1). The second form is a sample informed consent form for informants to sign (see figure 3.2 on pp. 31–32).

Prepare a 1–2 page document containing the following information:

1. the name of the microculture you have chosen (if appropriate, choose a pseudonym);
2. a two-line description of the informant (choose a pseudonym) and the person's role in the microculture;
3. the advantages presented by the microculture and the informant;
4. the disadvantages presented by the microculture and the informant (be candid— you will later incorporate this information into your methodology section of your final paper);
5. "Research with Human Participants Statement"

    a. What risks, if any, will the research pose to the informant?

    b. What risks, if any, will the research pose to you, the researcher? (Recall, if you will, the course requirement that you *not* study illegal cultural scenes! Consider issues of privacy, embarrassment, and harm to relationships.)

    c. If there are risks, how will they be minimized? (Consider the course requirement that you not reveal things in public that might harm your informant and your decision regarding the use of a pseudonym.)

    d. How will the anonymity of your informant be protected? (For instance, where will the interview data be stored? What safeguards will you put in place to insure that only you have access to interview material? Will you use a pseudonym throughout your transcribed interviews or only in materials that you show to the class?)

    e. How will you secure consent, i.e., how will you explain the project to your informant? (purpose of interviews, use of tape recorder, number and length of interviews, use of pseudonym, welcome to refuse to answer any questions that make him/her uncomfortable, right to withdraw from the project, etc.)

Figure 3.1   Writing a research proposal for submission to a review committee

Consent Form
[Insert title of study]

You are invited to be in a research study of [insert general statement about study]. You were selected as a possible participant because [explain how subject was identified]. We ask that you read this form [or read the form with a nonliterate informant] and ask any questions you may have before agreeing to be in the study.

This study is being conducted by: [Name and affiliation]

Background Information:

The purpose of this study is: [Explain research question and purpose in lay language.]

Procedures:

If you agree to participate in this part of the study, the interview will last [duration of interviews]. The interviews will feel like a conversation, where you will be asked some questions, and then encouraged to talk for as long as you like. The interview will be recorded on a tape recorder. Examples of questions are:

"Tell me how you usually start your day."

[Additional examples.]

(continued)

Others Involved in the Study:

[Who else is being asked to participate in this study.]

Risks and Benefits of Being in the Study:

[Sample description of risks and benefits: The worst problem from participating in this study is that you may feel that some questions are private. You are free to not answer any question. You do not have to talk about things unless you want to. You may stop the interview at any time. There may be no direct benefit for you for taking part in this study.]

Confidentiality:

[Sample description of use of data: The records of this study will be kept private. In any sort of published report, we will not include any information that will make it possible to identify anyone. Research records will be stored securely and only researchers will have access to the records. The tape recording of the interview will be transcribed and your name will be changed so that no one can identify you. The transcripts of the interview will be used to help researchers better understand the experiences of people (define goals of study here). The tapes will be erased after we have a paper copy of the transcript of the interview. The paper copy will not have your name on it. It will be kept for future research on this topic.]

Voluntary Nature of the Study:

Your decision whether or not to participate will not affect [describe any connections to informant and possible access to services.] You are free to not answer any question or withdraw at any time without affecting those relationships.

Contacts and Questions:

The researcher directing this study is: [Insert name and full contact information.]

You will be given a copy of this information to keep for your records.

Statement of Consent:

I have read the above information. If I had questions, I asked them and received answers to them. I consent to participate in the study.

Signature:_____   Date: _____

Signature of parent or guardian:_____   Date: _____
(If minors are involved)
Signature of Investigator:_____   Date: _____

Figure 3.2   Informed consent form *(continued)*

Discovering Folk Terms

Once you have chosen a microculture and found a willing cultural informant, you are ready to begin ethnographic research. You arrange to meet your informant in a place where you can talk easily and arrive to conduct your first interview. Now what do you do? If you were administering a survey, you would already have a list of prepared questions designed to measure something of scientific interest. You would explain this to your respondent and begin to ask her questions and record her answers.

But as an ethnographer, you are not conducting a survey; you are there to discover your informant's microculture. How do you explain this to your informant and what kinds of questions do you ask to elicit your informant's cultural knowledge? In this and the next two chapters, we will discuss the interviewing process, dividing the procedure into three basic steps: (1) discovering folk terms, (2) eliciting taxonomic structure, and (3) determining meaning. Each step is a task that involves different kinds of ethnographic questions, and as you become skilled at these tasks you can use all three kinds in a single interview depending on which ones seem most useful at the moment. To learn to ask ethnographic questions, however, we suggest that you begin with what we call *descriptive questions* and add new types of questions in subsequent interviews.

The First Interview

Before we discuss the actual interviewing process, we need to look at the setting for the first interview. Ideally, it is best to interview away from where the informant's culture takes place. This avoids interruptions and the influence of curious bystanders, bosses, and onlookers. Quiet helps as well since you will want to use a tape recorder. Unfortunately, ideal conditions may be impossible to find so you may need to improvise or put up with distractions. In any event, try to anticipate what effect the surroundings will have on you and your informant's comfort level and performance.

Explaining the Research

There is also the problem of how to explain the nature of ethnographic interviewing to your informant. Even if you described the project when you asked your informant to do the interviews, it is a good idea to again state what the interviews will be like. Most people don't know what a cultural anthropologist is or does, and, as we have noted before, based on their prior experience they will expect you to ask them about some topic or problem that *you* are interested in. They will expect direct questions, such as how old they are, where they were born, what their income is, and how they rate their job satisfaction.

But you won't be asking questions like these. Instead, because you seek to help them teach you their cultural knowledge, your questions will be more like those asked by someone who arrives at a new job. Like the first day on the job as a new employee, you will want to know where things are, what they are called, which people work there, what behavior is expected of you, what special problems you might face, and a host of other things that will help you learn to be a member of the group.

One way to start is to point out that interviews won't have questions like those on questionnaires or surveys. Then give a little history about ethnography. Say something like:

> In the past (and even today), anthropologists entered foreign societies to do fieldwork. They couldn't ask survey questions because they often didn't have any background knowledge about the people they came to live with. Instead, they had to learn the people's language and discover the knowledge the "locals" used when they engaged in daily life. They called this knowledge *culture*. Recently anthropologists have discovered that there are subgroups like yours [the informant's] that also have their own culture and ways to act and do things. It is important to know about them because this knowledge can prevent members of different subgroups from misunderstanding one another. In fact, anthropologists are often hired by companies

and the government to discover the cultural differences and sort out the misunderstandings.

With this "I want to discover what I would need to know to be a member of your group" approach, it might be useful to use the "new employee" analogy we discussed above. Ask your informant to imagine that she has to teach you how to be part of her culture. Liken the task to what she would do to help a new employee (or member of whatever group you are studying) become oriented to the surroundings, other group members, and tasks performed by the group members.

Finally, stress that she should answer your questions using words that she would normally employ with other members of her culture. (You do this because, as we will see next, you want to discover folk terms.) Also point out that she doesn't have to tell you anything that she is uncomfortable with and that there are no "right" answers. Always thank informants for doing the interview and note how helpful they have been.

There are actually many other ways ethnographers have explained their research to informants. Since ethnographic interviewing is a personal process, what you choose to say may depend on your social skills, prior experience, the nature of the microculture you have chosen, whether or not you already know the informant, or a host of other considerations. You may find it useful to talk about this or any problems you encounter during your research with classmates and instructors.

One thing we ask our students to do before they meet with an informant for the first time is to pair up with a classmate and take turns interviewing each other for twenty minutes. This not only provides some initial interviewing experience but also demonstrates what it is like to be an informant. Recently, we have had students videotape their practice interviews. Although it is sometimes painful to watch yourself perform, viewing the interview is a good way to assess your body language. Do you maintain eye contact with the informant? Do you look interested or bored?

Asking Descriptive Questions

Once you have made your introductions, discussed the research, obtained consent, and talked about recording the interview and taking notes, you must ask your first ethnographic question. To understand what that question (and other initial questions) is and the rationale for asking it, we need to look briefly at the theory behind ethnosemantic interviewing. (Useful sources on ethnosemantics include Spradley 1972; Tyler 1969; Casagrande and Hale 1967; Frake 1962; Goodenough 1956; Sturtevant 1964; Walker 1965; Werner and Schoepfle 1986.)

Cultural Categories. Ethnosemantic interviewing is based on the supposition that knowledge, including shared cultural knowledge, is

stored as a system of categories in the human brain. A *category* is a group
of things that people classify together and treat as if they were the same.
To create categories, people lump together closely related things on the
basis of shared attributes while ignoring their differences. For example,
we classify a certain set of actions in the game of tennis as a "serve." We
do so because we recognize that among other things, serves occur at
definable intervals during a game, are done with an overhead stroke, and
give the server an advantage over the opponent. But if you observe a tennis match closely, you will see that no two serves are exactly alike. Some
cause the ball to hit the net. The racket may be angled differently from
one serve to the next. The ball may exhibit a slightly different spin each
time it is hit. We overlook these differences and focus on the similarities
to create the category.

Categories *simplify* the world we apprehend with our senses or imagine in our minds. If we always focused on the unique features of everything we can sense, our world would consist of many more impressions
than we can store in our brains. By classifying slightly different things
together on the basis of some attributes they share, we create a manage-
able number of categories to use as we cope with the natural and social
worlds in which we live.

Folk Terms.   Cultural categories are part of an informant's knowledge but their existence can't be physically sensed. They are hidden in the
informant's brain and so far no way has been found to physically observe
them in this complex organ. Their existence must be inferred.

One way to infer them is to *observe* an informant's behavior, looking
for repetition, sequences, and associations, and to assume the patterns
that emerge represent cultural categories. As we noted in chapter 1, this is
the only way to get at tacit cultural categories, ones that are not coded in
language. Once they believe they have discovered tacit cultural categories,
researchers usually name them, and we call these kinds of names *analytical terms*. They are observer generated.

A second way to infer the existence of cultural categories is to discover the names informants give them. Luckily, although some categories
are tacit, as we have just noted, most categories are named; they represent
explicit culture because they are part of an informant's language. We con-
clude from this that if we can find the words that name things when informants talk with other members of their microculture, we can infer the
existence of the group's cultural categories. We call these informant-generated words *folk terms*. For example, when stockbrokers say words such
as *bull pen, cage, waffle, put, red herring*, and *dog and pony show* when they
speak to each other, they are using folk terms, and we infer that these folk
terms stand for cultural categories, although we may not know what they
mean yet.

There is one other kind of term we need to mention here, ***translation terms***. Translation terms are words that members of a group may use when they talk about their culture to outsiders. Such words are often general and are used to approximate the speaker's culture. For example, a tramp might use the word "sleep" when talking with a social worker who does not know his culture, but he would never use this translation term when he talks with other tramps. For them the folk term is *flop* and it has a much more precise meaning in tramp culture than "sleep" does.

A problem for ethnosemantic ethnographers is telling the difference between translation terms and folk terms. That is why we stress the need to regularly ask informants if the words they are giving us to describe their culture are the same ones they use with each other. The reason for eliciting folk terms is that they refer directly to folk categories. We figure that when members of a group use them, they know what they are talking about.

Spotting folk terms for English-speaking groups can be troublesome in another way. Many words used by members of a group are common to most English speakers. For example, brokers pick up their *mail*, a word we all commonly use. The term is still a folk term because members of broker culture use it to describe a category that has special meaning in their world. Unlike the mail most of us get, broker mail consists of *confirms, wires, red herrings,* and a variety of other pieces associated with brokerage business. It is easy to spot slang and technical speech associated with microcultures, but don't overlook other words that informants use when they talk with each other.

Design Features of Descriptive Questions. The discovery of folk terms is the first step in the ethnosemantic process. In the end, it is the discovery of how folk terms (and the categories they refer to) are organized and what they mean that gives us an understanding of a culture using this method. But what is the best way to find them?

There are two ways to discover folk terms. We could hang out near people belonging to a particular microculture and listen to them talk. This is not easy for many reasons, and it is a slow and unstructured approach. Instead, we believe it is most fruitful and efficient to elicit folk terms by *interviewing* informants. But the question still remains, what kinds of questions do you ask to achieve this goal?

The answer to this question involves the use of what we call descriptive questions. ***Descriptive questions*** are primarily intended to elicit folk terms. The idea behind them is to encourage informants to talk about their cultural worlds and in the process, to use folk terms. As their name suggests, they ask informants to describe things, such as events and places. Before we list them, we should mention some of the rules that go into their design.

- *Interview about what members of the microculture* do *and what things are called and look like,* not how informants *feel* about things or what things are *like.* (If you ask them what things are like, they are liable to use translation terms. If you ask how they "feel" about things you have focused the interview on them, not their culture.)

- *It is crucial to put the question in context.* The more context you can supply with a question, the easier it is for an informant to recall information. If someone were to ask you to describe life at your college or university, it would be hard for you to know where to begin. There are so many things you could talk about. What should you say? If the same person were to ask you what is the first thing you do when you get up on Tuesday morning at college, you should be able to answer easily. And the easier it is for informants to recall information, the more relaxed and confident they are likely to be, which also helps with rapport.

- *Avoid asking "what is a . . ." questions* such as, "What's a confirm?" or "What's a cage?" when you discover informants using folk terms. These ask for meaning and often lead informants on a tangent, interrupting the topic being described. You will have a chance to ask for meaning later when you use what we call attribute questions (see chapter 6). Meaning questions are especially difficult to avoid since it is natural to ask what things are in normal conversation.

- *Do not ask informants* why *they do something,* especially during the first few interviews. Questions such as, "Why do you need confirms?" and "Why do you bother to make cold calls?" ask for motivation and imply judgment on your part. You should avoid the impression that you are judging what you hear even if the judgment is positive.

Descriptive Questions

Now let's turn to the questions themselves. There are four kinds of descriptive questions: (1) grand tour questions, (2) mini tour questions, (3) story questions, and (4) native language check questions. Let us look at each giving examples and describing what they are good for.

Grand tour questions are the most general kind of descriptive question. This type of question is normally used as the first question you ask a new informant and may never be employed again. There are two kinds of grand tour questions based on what they ask informants to describe. The first asks for a description of *space*; it is literally a grand tour question. They look something like this (imagine we are interviewing a stockbroker).

- ◆ Could you take me on an imaginary tour of the office and point out everything I would see?
- ◆ Imagine I am blind. Could you describe what the office looks like for me?

The second kind of grand tour question asks for *action*. For example, you might ask:

- ◆ Could you describe what a stockbroker does during an average day here at the office from the time you arrive until you leave?

Mini tour questions are descriptive questions that ask for more detail about a folk term you have already discovered. They provide greater detail and a fuller picture of the informant's world. For example, suppose when you asked your informant to tell you about his average day at the office, he mentioned that he makes *cold calls* or works in *the bull pen*. You might ask mini tour questions like these:

- ◆ Could you describe how you make cold calls?
- ◆ Could you describe what the bull pen looks like for me?

Mini tour questions are always based on folk terms you have learned from responses to earlier questions. We suggest you listen especially carefully for terms describing actions, such as *making cold calls*, as the interview progresses, because actions generate the fullest answers. To think of mini tour questions during an interview, it helps to write down action terms as you hear them.

Box 4.1   Interviewing Hint: The Repeating Strategy

Some informants find it difficult to describe things in detail. Their answers seem short and relatively unhelpful. Is there any way to encourage more expansive descriptive responses? A number of things may help. As noted above, informants tend to relax and say more when questions become more specific. Time helps, too, as informants get to know you better.

But there is one strategy that can also make a difference: repeating words your informant says. The strategy is borrowed from counseling and seems helpful in ethnographic interviewing because it indicates interest and an effort to understand what is being said on the anthropologist's part. Neutral interest seems to encourage expansiveness.

An example of repeating might look something like this.

BROKER: Then after I check my mail I go sit down in my cubicle and look at it [the mail] to see if there is anything important. Then I read the headlines in the *Wall Street Journal* and since I am pretty new here I will make some cold calls.

INTERVIEWER: I see, cold call.

BROKER: Yes, that is when I call prospects for the first, and maybe only [laugh] time, and then I check what the analysts have to say and look for investment ideas.

INTERVIEWER: Investment ideas?

BROKER: Yes, you need investment ideas to talk to your clients about. . . .

Story questions ask informants to tell you about actual events or places associated with their microculture. One story question would look like this:

◆ Could you tell me about the last time you made cold calls?

Stories are often loaded with detail and additional folk terms and are very useful for illustrating points when you write. We should point out that the accuracy of a story—whether or not events happened exactly the way an informant says they did—is not at issue here. People often differ in their recollections of events. What is important is the cultural content of stories since people tell stories using appropriate cultural categories and rules for action.

Native language questions are a kind of descriptive question designed to check whether or not a particular term is really a folk term. Native language questions check to see if a term given to you by your informant is one the informant normally uses with other members of the cultural group. For example, if an informant says, "Then we come in the *main room* here where most of the brokers work," you might ask the native language question:

◆ Do you call this the *main room* when you talk with other brokers?

The broker's answer should be, "No, not really. We actually call this the *bull pen*."

Native language questions help to insure that the terms you have discovered are actual folk terms, not translations or approximations.

Field Notes

Interviews should result in a set of *field notes*, which are written accounts of what transpired. If you tape recorded the interview, your field notes should consist of a typed transcription of everything that was said, including your questions. You might also want to add observations about how the interview went—was your informant nervous? What problems did you encounter? What worked? What kinds of questions did you ask? Did they work? You also should try to remember and record anything that was said when the tape recorder was off.

Typing field notes is a long and arduous process, but having a verbatim account of your informant's words is important to the cultural discovery process defined by the ethnosemantic method.

You may find it impractical to use a tape recorder all of the time or even at all. If this happens, try to jot down folk terms as you hear them, and as soon as possible after an interview is over, type—preferably on a computer for easy storage and retrieval—as detailed an account of the interview as possible. Be sure and make copies of your field notes (either printed or saved on a disk). There is nothing worse than losing notes you have just spent hours preparing.

Preliminary Analysis

When you have completed typing your field notes, look them over to identify folk terms. Some of our students have used different colored highlighter pens to identify folk nouns, phrases, and verbs. It may be useful to list topics covered in the interview in the margins of your notes. Think about possible mini tour questions you can ask during your next interview. What terms should be checked with a native language question? Finally, are there preliminary sets of terms that might form lists? This last question leads us to the discussion of taxonomic structure in chapter 5.

Discovering
Taxonomic Structure

What do you do next in the ethnographic research process once you have completed your first interview and typed your field notes? You can (and should) continue to ask descriptive questions during your second interview based on what you learned from the first encounter. But you should also move on to the next ethnographic step, *discovering taxonomic structure*. This chapter discusses the nature of taxonomies, why they are ethnographically useful, and the ethnographic questions used to discover them.

Taxonomic Structure

Domains

In the last chapter we argued that cultural categories are represented by words called *folk terms* and that the first ethnographic step is to discover some of them. But if you look closely at the folk terms you elicit, you will discover another feature of human knowledge; some categories are larger than others. Put another way, some categories categorize other categories.

It is easy to demonstrate this feature of knowledge. Just look at a parking lot and name the machines you see there. Most of you should say you see *cars*, although you may also spot some *motorcycles*, or *pickup trucks*.

All of these folk terms are categories, but all display another feature—
they are broader. They cover or include a number of other more specific
categories. The cars you see in the lot can be subdivided into categories
such as *Chevrolets, Hondas, Dodges,* and a variety of other more specific categories that are also represented by folk terms. These, in turn, can be subdivided. Hondas, for example, include *Accords, Civics, Del Sols,* and
Elements. Chevrolets include *Malibus, Impalas, Tahoes, Suburbans,* and
Astros. We call categories that categorize other categories **domains** and the
words that name them **cover terms**. The categories they classify now
become *included categories* or *subcategories.*

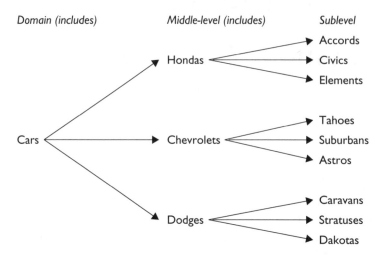

Figure 5.1   Diagram of a domain and subcategories

Domains include subcategories linguistically, meaning that the
domain word (cover term) can be used to *name* the subcategories. Take
money for example. You might say when you are about to visit your local
bank, "I am going to go to the bank to deposit some money." A friend
might ask, "Oh, are you just depositing checks or are you also going to
put in some cash?" In this case, the cover term *money* is used to name both
checks and *cash.* Money is a broader term that can be used to include
(lump together) smaller terms (subcategories) as people speak. We call
this verbal arrangement **semantic inclusion**.

Taxonomies

The sets of terms along with the domains that include them are called
taxonomies. Taxonomies are simply lists of different things that are classi-

fied together under a domain word by members of a microculture on the basis of some shared certain attributes. The term *taxonomy* is also used to refer to the *box chart* that displays sets of included categories. For example, the taxonomy of kinds of money described above would look like this.

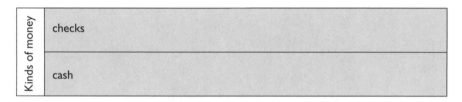

Figure 5.2 Simple taxonomy of kinds of money

Note that we place the domain term in the box to the left, and each included term in its own box on the right to indicate that the domain semantically "covers" (can be used to refer to) the included terms.

Taxonomies may have only two levels (the domain and one set of included terms) as indicated in figure 5.2, or more than two as illustrated in figure 5.3. For example, we have noted that the term *money* semantically can be used to refer to the term *cash*. But we also talk about *coins* (alternately known as *change*) and *bills*. Coins and bills are kinds of cash; both can be referred to by that single term or even more generally as a kind of money.

But there are also kinds of coins and bills. Coins can include pennies, nickels, dimes, quarters, fifty-cent pieces, and dollars. Bills include ones, fives, tens, twenties, fifties, hundreds, five hundreds, and thousands. When we take this information into consideration, the taxonomy in figure 5.2 has expanded into one with four levels (see figure 5.3 on p. 46). There are a few other things to note about multilevel taxonomies. First, we call the categories found on intermediate levels *middle-level categories.* Second, middle-level categories can only be used in speech to name the categories that fall under them. Fives are a kind of bill; quarters are a kind of coin. Fives are not, however, a kind of coin.

Box 5.1 Making Taxonomic Boxes on the Computer

It is possible to make taxonomic box charts using the tables feature of word processing programs such as MSWord and WordPerfect. Use the "merge cells" feature to erase the rows to create larger boxes. We prefer making the tables in a word processing program rather than a spreadsheet program, e.g. Excel, to facilitate inserting charts directly into the text of the final ethnography.

checks			
cash	coins		pennies
			nickels
			dimes
			quarters
			fifty-cent pieces
			dollars
	bills		ones
			twos
			fives
			tens
			twenties
			fifties
			hundreds (C-notes)
			five hundreds
			thousands

(Kinds of money)

Level 1 (includes)   Level 2 (includes)   Level 3 (includes)   Level 4
(Domain)   (Middle-Level Categories)

Figure 5.3   Expanded taxonomy of kinds of money

There is one more thing to mention about categories represented in a taxonomy. The same category may have more than one name. We call multiple names for the same category *alternates* of that category. *Twenties*, for example, can also be called *twenty dollar bills*. *Hundreds* can be referred to as *C-notes*. We suggest that you primarily use the most common term for a category and if you wish to state its alternates, put them in parentheses as indicated for hundreds in figure 5.3.

Semantic Relationships

If you look closely at figures 5.2 and 5.3, you will notice that the domain cover terms are not stated as a single word. For example, instead of *money*, the domain reads "kinds of *money*." The phrase "kinds of" represents what is called a ***semantic relationship***. Semantic relationships state the basis on which subcategories are included by a domain term. In figures 5.2 and 5.3, cash and checks are *kinds of* money.

Technically, all taxonomies are built around the "kinds of" or strict inclusion semantic relationship. But it is possible to add attributes to the kinds of relationship to create additional useful semantic relationships.

For example, we often use a "ways to" semantic relationship to generate taxonomies. This elicits lists of actions more easily. Technically, "ways to" is actually "kinds of ways to" but we leave off the "kinds of" when we use it. An example might be "studying hard is a way to get an A in cultural anthropology." Figure 5.4 is a chart of four of the most useful semantic relationships.

Kind of relationship	Relational diagram	Relational statement	Example
Strict inclusion	X is *a kind of* Y	"kinds of"	a dime is a kind of coin
Sequence	X is *a step in* Y	"steps in"	stopping a vehicle is a step in hitchhiking
Part-Whole	X is *a part of* Y	"parts of"	a wheel is part of a car
Means-End	X is *a way to do* Y	"way to"	using Honda cleaner/polish is a way to shine your motorcycle

Figure 5.4   Semantic relationships

Design Principles of a Taxonomy

When you begin to make taxonomies, you will find that it is easy to run into problems. To avoid trouble, it is useful to keep the four-level design principles in mind as you look them over, then ask yourself if the taxonomy meets all of the five requirements listed below.

- *Hierarchy:* Taxonomies are hierarchies of terms; the more general ones cover the more specific ones.
- *Inclusion:* Taxonomic hierarchies are constructed on the principle of semantic inclusion, as we have already noted. That means that more general terms are used to refer to the lower-level terms members of a microculture include in their everyday language.

A common mistake to make when working with folk taxonomies (meaning ones made from folk terms) is to list subterms under a cover term based on shared attributes, not how people speak. At the midwestern college where we teach, for example, student informants will sometimes classify *language houses* as dormitories when you ask them because both language houses and dormitories repre-

sent places where students reside. But when students speak to each
other, they do not call language houses dormitories. They are two
separate domains.

- *Folk language validity:* The taxonomies you create are folk taxonomies. That means they must contain the actual words, folk terms,
that people use when speaking to each other in their microcultural
context. Ideally, once you have created a taxonomy you should
show it to your informant and ask if every word there is one used
by members of the microculture in daily conversation.

- *Single relationship of inclusion:* A taxonomy must have a single
semantic relationship of inclusion throughout. That means that all
the subcategories found in a "kinds of" taxonomy, for example,
must be included as kinds of the higher categories and domain. It is
really easy for informants to shift relationships when you are eliciting terms for a taxonomy, so watch out. For example you might be
collecting a taxonomy of kinds of motorcycles such as Hondas,
Harley Davidsons, and Suzukis only to find your informant start to
list wheels, carburetors, and handlebars as well. Informants may do
this because wheels and carburetors are related to motorcycles. But
without knowing it, he has shifted the semantic relationship from
kinds of motorcycles to *parts of* motorcycles.

- *Contrast on the same taxonomic level:* The folk terms listed on the same
level in a taxonomy must contrast with each other. This means they
cannot refer to the same category or be the same thing. If you ask
an informant, she will tell you that a dollar bill is not the same as a
twenty dollar bill. These two categories contrast with each other.
Once again, the way to check for contrast is to show the taxonomy
to your informant and ask if any of the terms on the same level are
or could be the same.

Eliciting Taxonomies

Eliciting taxonomies involves two tasks: analyzing your field notes
for partial taxonomies and asking structural questions. Let us look at
each of these steps.

Step 1: Analyzing Field Notes

The first step to take when you wish to elicit categories that form a
taxonomy is to look for partial taxonomies, or at least domains, in your
field notes. Imagine you are interviewing a member of the Gold Wing
Road Riders Association (GWRRA; GW for short), a national associa-

tion with (at this writing) 85,000 members divided into regions, districts (states), and local chapters. Since members of the GW can't describe an average day associated with this microculture (members don't congregate on a day-to-day basis), you first ask about the social situations (*events* in their language) where GW members get together. Your informant gives you a short list of events (a taxonomy in itself), including one called the *district rally*. You choose that social situation as the subject for your first grand tour question and the exchange goes like this: [*Actions are in boldface, domains are in bold italics, subcategories are in italics.*]

> **Q.** You mentioned that one of the events you attend is called a district rally. Could you please describe what people do at a rally from the time they get there until they leave?
>
> **A.** Well sure. The ***rally*** starts on Thursday although a lot of people can't make it before Friday . . . or even Saturday . . . because they work. We usually **stay at the motel** that has been reserved for the rally. Some people **camp** or stay at other motels too but we like to be where the action is so we stay at the ***host motel***. We **ride** there on our ***Wings***, arrive, check in, and **unload** our bikes. ***Gold Wings*** have *side bags* and a *trunk* that holds a lot of stuff and then most of the members tow *trailers* packed with stuff too. Then . . . let's see . . . we go to our rooms. I always change out of my ***riding gear*** and put on my *vest* before I go down and see everyone. Anyhow, we go down, **register** for the rally, get our ***pins*** and maybe ***hangers*** out of the *registration packet* and put them on, and maybe **buy** some *50-50 tickets* for the afternoon **drawing**. Then usually we go look at what ***vendors*** are there and what they are selling and at the ***booths*** to see what they are **raffling off**. If our ***chapter*** is responsible for some job, like **registering people** or **running the booths**, I might do that.

The first thing to do with transcribed notes is identify the most obvious folk terms in them. (Folk terms in the example above appear in either italics, boldface, or both.) Then make a list of verbs or actions. Later, you can ask mini tour questions about these (Could you describe what you do when you camp? for example) or place them in a list (taxonomy) tentatively labeled "Things you do when you go to a rally." In the example above, *registering people, running the booths, drawing, staying at a motel,* and *camping* (indicated in boldface) are verbs that might go in that list.

Now make a list of partial taxonomies you think are implied by your informant's folk terms. The list should like something like this for the interview transcribed above.

Kinds of Gold Wings
Kinds of pins
Kinds of hangers
Kinds of riding gear

Kinds of jobs
  Registering people
  Running the booths
Kinds of vendors
Kinds of things in the registration packet

Step 2: Asking Structural Questions

When you have completed a list of partial taxonomies, you need to discover if they contain additional folk terms. To do this, we use ***structural questions***, the kind of questions that elicit taxonomic categories. There are two kinds of structural questions: descending structural questions and ascending structural questions.

Descending structural questions are designed to elicit the *subcategories* of a domain. They are used when you have a domain term and a semantic relationship. The two questions below are good examples:

◆ You mentioned that there were Gold Wings at the rally. What kinds of Gold Wings are there?

◆ You mentioned that GW members do several things at a rally. What are the things GW members do at a district rally?

The first question illustrated above should yield names of Gold Wing motorcycles, such as *1000s, 1100s,* and *1500s.* (Note that we italicize folk terms when we use them in text.) The second question should produce things GWs do at the rally, such as *eat, go on poker runs, enter the bike show, do bike games, look at accessories, see how other members decorate and accessorize their bikes, talk about summer trips, take dinner runs,* and a host of other activities. As you collect subcategories, put them in a taxonomic box diagram like the ones shown earlier.

Ascending structural questions are designed to discover domain or *higher-level categories.* Put another way, if you have discovered some categories that all appear to be on the same level and are listed together by your informant, you ask what they are all called. For example:

◆ You mentioned 1000s, 1100s, and 1500s. Are they all kinds of something?

◆ You take leaf runs, dinner runs, breakfast runs, and bug runs. Are these all called something?

As you might guess, the answer to the first question should be kinds of *Gold Wings* and to the second question, kinds of *runs.*

There are four more points to remember when using structural questions to elicit taxonomies.

1. Repeat what you have already learned before you ask for more subcategories. Thus, you would say, "You mentioned that there are

leaf runs, Dairy Queen runs, bug runs, dinner runs, and breakfast runs. Are there any other kinds of runs?"

2. Reassure informants when they can't think of anything more to go in a taxonomy. Sometimes informants believe there are more subcategories but they can't think of them. Reassure them by saying they shouldn't worry; if they think of any more they can tell you later, and indeed, they often do.

3. Ask native language check questions as you collect terms for a taxonomy.

4. Stay with the same structural question until you have collected all taxonomic subcategories your informant can remember. Informants often want to explain what things mean as they are listing them. Explanations of meaning often redirect the interview away from the listing process. A little side explanation is acceptable and part of normal speech, but too much leads you off task. At this point you don't need to know what things mean, you need to fill out taxonomies.

Troubleshooting for Errors in Taxonomies

Taxonomies sound easy enough to construct, but everyone who uses them has experienced trouble with them from time to time. There are at least four things that should *not* happen in a taxonomy.

1. Terms should not occur twice.

2. There should not be only one term listed under one term. Listing a single term implies that it is the same as the term in the category above it.

3. There should be no empty boxes. An empty box implies there should be a term there.

4. There should be no categories that cannot be referred to by the domain category.

Bad Spots

Some taxonomies look fine overall, but have a bad spot (problem area) in them. This is often indicated by an empty box or one term included by the exact same term on the level above it.

The classification of Gold Wing 1200 motorcycles follows this pattern. *Gold Wing 1200s* can be divided into *Interstates, Aspencades*, and *SEs*. But Honda also made a basic Gold Wing they simply refer to as a Gold Wing 1200. The taxonomic diagram displays a repeated term in this case, indicating that a Gold Wing 1200 is a Gold Wing 1200. The best way to explain this is that the first-level Gold Wing 1200 has a more general scope (it includes all the rest) than the Gold Wing 1200 on the second level. In essence, they mean slightly different things. In this case, you can leave the repeated word in the taxonomy.

Kinds of Gold Wing 1200s	Gold Wing 1200
	Interstate
	Aspencade
	SE

Figure 5.5   Simple taxonomy of kinds of Gold Wing 1200s

Compound Taxonomies

Occasionally you and your informant will produce a taxonomy (usually large with three or four levels) that is a complete mess. Terms repeat not just in one place, but everywhere and on different levels. Things can be kinds of each other. The clearest signs of a compound taxonomy are repeated categories and sets of terms that cannot be included semantically by the domain cover term (see figure 5.6). They usually come about for two reasons: the first is a desire on the ethnographer's or informant's part to jam everything about a topic into one taxonomy.

Kinds of Gold Wing 1200s	Interstate	blue red gold silver
	Aspencade	blue gray silver green
	SE	purple silver gold black

Figure 5.6   Compound taxonomy of kinds of Gold Wing 1200s

In this case, the third level of the taxonomy does not contain kinds of Gold Wing 1200s. The term "blue Interstate" may designate a particular motorcycle in a parking lot, but it is not used as the name of a kind of GW1200 when riders speak with each other about them. Instead, the color terms represent a taxonomy called "kinds of Gold Wing 1200 colors." To "clean up" the taxonomy, either make it into two taxonomies or eliminate the third level.

The second kind of messy compound taxonomy is also marked by the presence of repeated terms and confused levels, but all the terms are folk terms that are "covered" (are named) by the domain. Using the example of money, this kind of compound taxonomy appears in figure 5.7. Bank tellers refer to all the terms in figure 5.7 as folk terms covered by the domain, *kinds of money*. They say things like, "Did you spot any counterfeit money?" or "I haven't got enough ones," or "Do you want to send me up the new fives?" During an interview tellers will claim that all these terms are kinds of money.

Kinds of money			
ones	old		
	new		
twos			
fives	old		
	new		
tens	old		
	new		
twenties	old		
	new	real	
		counterfeit	
fifties	real		
	counterfeit		
hundreds	real		
	counterfeit		
five hundreds			
thousands			
old	ones		
	fives		
	tens		
	twenties		
new			
counterfeit			
real			

Figure 5.7 Compound taxonomy of kinds of money

But if you try to put all these terms in a single taxonomy it soon becomes clear that they can become kinds of each in a haphazard way, and that there is terminological repetition almost everywhere. What is going on?

The answer seems to be that there is more than one way to classify kinds of money and these different classifications (actually separate taxonomies each covered by the same domain term) are used in different social settings. The most common one, and the one you ought to use as the primary taxonomy, is based on the formal name of each kind of money, one that reflects the denominations of each bill. Less common are two smaller taxonomies, one based on whether or not the bills are real and the other based on what shape they are in.

Our recommendation is to use the largest set of categories (the one that seems most like a set of formal names and that informants feel "go together") as the basis for a taxonomy, and to either display the remaining small taxonomies in separate charts or use them as dimensions of contrast in a paradigm. (Dimensions of contrast and paradigms are discussed in chapter 6.) Either way, you won't lose the information contained in the smaller taxonomies.

Why Collect Taxonomies?

Taxonomies are ethnographically useful, even essential, for several reasons. First, they yield an added sense of how members of a group order or structure their cultural knowledge. This structure is as much a part of culture as are cultural categories themselves.

Second, eliciting taxonomies yields more detailed and exhaustive data than does asking less directed or more general questions, and it does so in less time.

Third, taxonomic lists are essential to the discovery of detailed cultural *meaning,* as we will see in the next chapter. They contain sets of contrasting terms, and it is by exploiting this contrast that we can discover the attributes that give each term meaning. Using the principle of contrast is so important for the discovery of detailed meaning that we suggest you do not ask what things mean while you are collecting folk terms and taxonomies. Wait until you have contrast sets to help you generate detailed meaning.

Fourth, it is difficult for informants to remember what they know about their own cultures. Our culture becomes so routine and usual that most of us are unaware of the categories that guide our actions and interpretations. Taxonomies produce lists of closely associated categories, and, as memory experts have argued for decades, associating one category with another is a key to remembering them. When you ask informants to list taxonomic subcategories the natural association of the terms helps jog their memories. On many occasions we have had informants come back to us after an interview saying, "Oh, I thought of three more things that are kinds of X."

Finally, taxonomies provide illustrations and occasionally the structure of final ethnographic reports.

Discovering Meaning

Up to this point we have advised you not to ask your informants about what things mean. Instead, we have had you focus on discovering folk terms and eliciting their taxonomic structure. In this chapter, we finally turn to the discovery of meaning. We held off doing so until now because we believe it is essential to uncover meaning in *detail*, and the method we suggest that you use to do this depends on the collection of taxonomies. Taxonomies yield lists of terms we call contrast sets. When informants compare terms in a contrast set, they (the informants) usually provide more detail about the differences and similarities among the terms than they would if you simply asked them to define each folk term separately.

In this chapter, we look at the nature of cultural meaning, introduce the concept of attribution, stress the importance of limited contrasts, show how to find contrast sets, discuss how to construct paradigms (our word for the comparative chart used to display attributional meaning), and ask ethnographic questions called "attribute questions" that are used to generate attributional meaning.

Attributional Meaning

We believe that the total *meaning* of any cultural category consists of all the shared categories it is related to in the minds of microcultural members and the relationships that bind them to the category being defined. We call these related categories *attributes,* and the category being defined along with its cluster of attributes a *folk concept.*

Think of the meaning of any particular category as a cluster. The category is in the center of the cluster; the attributes that give it meaning are arranged around it connected by relationship lines. For example, one of the authors (McCurdy) rides a Honda *Gold Wing* motorcycle. If you are familiar with the world of transportation you may have some idea what Gold Wing means (for example, one of its attributes is that it is kind of motorcycle), but many of you may find the term a mystery.

If you were studying members of the Gold Wing Road Riders Association (GW), the meaning of Gold Wing runs even deeper since they define it by many different attributes. If you interview GW members you would discover that Gold Wings built in 2004 are *touring machines.* They have *six cylinders* in a *boxer* or *flat configuration.* They are *heavy bikes* ("bikes" is an alternate term for motorcycle in this culture), have *shaft drives, lots of on-board luggage space, cruise control, a full fairing, windshield, automatic turn signal canceller, comfortable seat, two-up* (two people) *capacity, good handling at speed, mechanical reliability, smooth transmission,* and a *quiet, vibrationless,* and *powerful* engine. They are also *expensive* (about $18,500 in 2004) and owned by *older, clean-cut* riders.

And these are just a few of the attributes GW members associate with their Gold Wings. In short, a machine that most people who are nonowners will simply think of as a large motorcycle covered with lots of streamlined plastic panels has a much richer meaning in the microculture of a group that formed an association around it. That meaning stems from all the attributes Gold Wing riders associate with the motorcycle. (See figure 6.1 for a partial attribute cluster that defines the "Gold Wing" concept.)

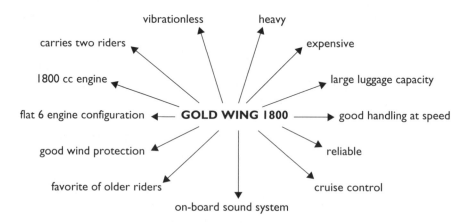

Figure 6.1   Diagram of a partial attribute cluster (there are many more attributes than are shown here)

Discovering and Displaying Attributional Meaning

But how can you discover the attributes that give a category its meaning? One way is to do what many professional anthropologists do: hang out with informants for long periods of time, listening to them talk and watching what they do. If you do this long enough and take good field notes, you will learn and record a number of attributes of a variety of folk categories. Since most of you will not have time to "hang out" like this, there is an interviewing approach to the discovery of attributional meaning that is usually efficient and structured. We call this approach *attributional* (sometimes also called *componential*) *analysis*. This approach involves several steps, including the identification of contrast sets, setting up a paradigm chart in which to record attributes, checking previous interviews for attributes and using them to create dimensions of contrast, and using attribute questions to find new dimensions of contrast and fill out partial ones. Let us discuss each of these in turn.

Identifying Contrast Sets

Attributional analysis depends on the principle of *contrast*, specifically *partial contrast*. The *principle of partial contrast* basically says you can discover more attributes of something if you ask informants to compare it to something else that is nearly like it. The *partial* in partial contrast refers to this close relationship between different categories, since closely related categories will share many attributes. If you were to ask informants to compare categories that are in complete contrast (completely different), they will tend to give you the most general attributes. But if you ask informants to compare Honda Gold Wings with Harley Davidson FLHT Electra Glides, you are asking a question that employs the principle of partial contrast—both are motorcycles used for long distance touring but are still different in a number of detailed ways that are important to motorcycle owners who tour.

Where can you find sets of terms that are in partial contrast? The answer is, in taxonomies. The taxonomies you have collected in your initial interviews consist of lists of closely related terms, thus categories in partial contrast. (This is why one of the taxonomic design principles we discussed in chapter 5 states that terms on the same level in a taxonomy must be different—i.e., be in contrast—from each other.)

Thus, the first step in doing attributional analysis is to identify the sets of terms that are in partial contrast in taxonomies. We call these groups contrast sets. A *contrast set* is any set of categories found in a taxonomy that are included by the term just above it (the next highest category that semantically includes the terms). In a two-level taxonomy (a two-level taxonomy, remember, consists of a domain and the single list of included terms that appear under it), there is only one contrast set. The list in the shaded area shown in figure 6.2 is a contrast set. The data used to make the set was collected from a GW member in 1998 for models built that year. The question mark indicates there are possibly more categories to go in the taxonomy.

Kinds of Luxo-Tourers	GL1500
	K1200RS
	Voyager XII
	FLHT
	?

Figure 6.2   Contrast set in a partial two-level taxonomy

For a taxonomy of three or more levels, there will be two or more contrast sets. One contrast set is always the second level of the taxonomy but a third level will contain at least one, and often more than one, contrast set as is illustrated in figure 6.3. (The lightly shaded area is the second level contrast set. The two more darkly shaded areas are two additional contrast sets found on the third level.)

Constructing a Paradigm

The next step in attributional analysis is to create a matrix, which we call a *paradigm,* that includes a contrast set you have chosen to sort for attributional meaning. Your first challenge is to choose a contrast set that seems useful. This requires judgment on your part and the decision is

Kinds of Luxo-Tourers	GL1500	SE Aspencade
	K1200RS	
	Voyager XII	
	FLHT	FLHT FLHTC El Gold Classic FLHTCI El Gold Classic EFI FLHTCUI UI Classic EG-FI

Figure 6.3   Contrast sets in a partial three-level taxonomy

often based on the extent to which a contrast set *appears* (to you or your informant) to be useful as a way to comprehend the microculture you are trying to understand.

Take the three-level taxonomy depicted in figure 6.3. If the microculture of interest is Harley Davidson microculture, then it might be useful to sort the different kinds of FLHTs (Electra Glides). The meanings of different FLHT models are important to Harley riders. If you are interviewing a member of the Gold Wing Road Riders as we did some years ago, differences among kinds of FLHTs are less important. The GL1500 models are more important, but of even greater interest is how GW members assign attributes to different touring motorcycles since the discovery of these attributes will likely say something about how they identify themselves in the motorcycle touring world and reveal some of the important factors that shape many parts of their culture.

To create a paradigm, place the contrast set in the left-hand column of the matrix. The paradigm will then consist mostly of empty boxes as depicted in figure 6.4 below.

Luxo-Tourers							
GL1500							
K1200RS							
Voyager XII							
FLHT							

Figure 6.4   Empty matrix for recording attributional data

Checking for Attributes in Your Field Notes

Step three involves an analysis of your field notes before your next informant interview. The reason for doing so is that informants invariably volunteer explanations of what things mean when you ask them descriptive and structural questions. The quote reproduced below from a 1998 interview with a GW informant illustrates this fact.

> This year I was thinking of buying a new bike. You know I like to tour, and I have been riding an '82 Interstate for sixteen years now. It's a good bike but a couple of guys I know kind of liked the looks of that BMW K bike [K1200RS] that's out too. So I thought, what the hell, I'll go over to GP Motorsports—that's the BMW dealer—and see if they got a demo to ride. And they did and I took it out for a ride. It didn't handle parking lot speeds so good but it was real quick

on the River Road curves and went fine on the interstate. But the
engine has a high pitch vibration up around 65 and I don't like that
and I didn't like the seat or the riding position, which is kind of bent
over, much. So if I pop for a new bike, and I think I got my wife
talked into it, it will be a Honda again, especially since they came out
with the 1500, which the guys really like.

At first glance this quote may seem like just another story, but actually it contains valuable attributional information that can be used to start
filling out a paradigm. Most of the information is about the BMW K bike,
but as you will see below, the points of comparison that are mentioned
can also be applied to other touring motorcycles. A list of attributes from
this quote looks like this:

Poor handling at slow speed
Great handling on curvy roads (River Road)
Good handling on the interstate
High pitch vibration at cruising speed
Uncomfortable seat
Uncomfortable riding position

Once you identify the attributes in your field notes, you can enter them
in the paradigm you are creating as partial dimensions of contrast. Think
of *dimensions of contrast* as points of comparison on which all the categories in the contrast set can be sorted. Incidentally, there is nothing unusual
about paradigms. *Consumer Reports* uses them to compare products they
are rating and so do many other magazines that rate products. The difference is that you are creating a *folk paradigm*. This means the dimensions of
contrast are given to you by your informants, not imposed on the analysis
by magazine editors. Figure 6.5 illustrates how to enter attributes in partial
dimensions of contrast in your paradigm. We have shaded one completed
dimension of contrast to indicate how it should look and boldfaced the
titles of other dimensions we were able to identify from our notes.

Once you have identified some of the dimensions of contrast and
entered them in the paradigm, you can ask your informant to fill in the

Luxo-Tourers	handling at slow speed	vibration	seat comfort	riding position	etc.
GL1500	fair to OK				
K1200RS	somewhat heavy feel	high-pitched	fair	less comfortable	
Voyager XII	heavy feel				
FLHT	heavy feel				

Figure 6.5   Partial paradigm of kinds of luxo-tourers

blanks. Ask your informant something like, "You said that the K1200RS didn't handle so well in the parking lot. How about the other bikes on the list?" The informant quoted above was able to do this for all the dimensions of contrast although he was least confident about the Voyager since he had only heard about it, not driven it.

Asking Attribute Questions

The next step in making a paradigm requires you to ask attribute questions. As the name suggests, *attribute questions* are ethnographic questions designed to elicit attributes. We suggest that you use any of four different attribute questions and/or two attribute tasks to elicit attributes. Before you start, however, it is a good idea to write each of the categories that form a contrast set on separate 3 × 5 cards and lay them out in front of the informant. This encourages informants to compare categories as they try to think of attributes when you ask them any kind of attribute question.

Attribute questions are the most formal questions you can ask an informant, so experiment with different kinds of questions and look for ways to put informants at ease when you use them. Remind the informant that there are no correct answers to these questions; informants are the bosses when it comes to what their folk terms mean. We will now take a closer look at atrribute questions and tasks.

Kinds of Attribute Questions. The four kinds of attribute questions include *definition questions, comparison questions, triadic sorting questions,* and *judgment questions.*

Definition questions ask an informant to tell you what a *single* category means. An example would be:

◆ You listed GL1500s here as luxo-tourers. What are they?

The informant will probably say something about the fact that GL1500s are big Honda touring machines and that they carry two people easily. Both are useful attributes of the machine. But you are less likely to discover many detailed attributes because the question does not require the informant to compare GL1500s with anything else. The next three kinds of questions remedy this deficiency.

Comparison questions ask your informant to compare two of the categories in the contrast set. For example, you might ask:

◆ Take the K1200RS and the GL1500. Can you tell me how they are different from each other?

Hopefully, the comparison will prompt the informant to expand the amount of detailed information he gives you. For example, he might point out that the GL is slightly bigger and heavier, that it has six cylinders, not four like the K bike, and that it gives more wind protection to the rider, all useful dimensions of contrast.

Triadic sorting questions are similar to comparison questions, but they ask the informant to compare three, not two, categories from the contrast set and to convey what is different and alike about them. For example, you might ask:

◆ Take the GL1500, K1200RS, and the FLHT. Which two are most alike and how do they differ from the third?

Your informant might say, "Well, the GL and the K bike are more alike because they both are water cooled while the Harley is air cooled." The informant might also note that the GL and K bike have shaft drives while the Harley uses a belt drive. The Harley and GL could be more alike, on the other hand, because both are more massive, less agile motorcycles on "twisty" roads. An informant might also say they are *all* alike in some ways or *all* different in some ways. The "ways" here amount to different dimensions of contrast.

Judgment questions ask your informant to tell you which category in the contrast set is best. (Note that we have told you not to ask for opinions when you asked descriptive or structural questions, but now is your chance.) For touring bikes you might ask:

◆ Look at these four kinds of tourers. Which one would you say is best?

Your informant may answer this question without hesitation, saying something like, "GL1500s are best. They are great long distance machines. They carry two-up better and have great torque and the most luggage capacity." Again you will have discovered several important dimensions of contrast with this question, and the answers should be significant to the informant since he is using them to make the judgment.

Sometimes an informant will respond with something like, "It all depends." When an informant gives this answer, simply ask, "What might it depend on?" He might answer, "Well, if you don't like vibration, the GL1500 is for you. It's so smooth and quiet that you sometimes have to look at the tach [tachometer] to see if it's running. The K bike and Voyager have a buzzy vibration at speed and the Harley vibrates the most but at a lower rate." Again the answer reveals an important dimension of contrast about the bikes' amount of vibration. You can go on to ask your informant if there are any other ways a bike could be best until your informant runs out of answers.

Attribute Tasks. There are also two tasks, twenty questions and card sorting, that you can ask your informant to do that may yield dimensions of contrast.

• *Twenty Questions:* Tell your informant that you are thinking of one of the categories in the contrast set and tell him to ask you questions to identify which one it is. When you say this about the motorcycle contrast set your informant might ask something like, "Does it have shaft drive?" Since you don't know which motorcycles have a shaft drive you ask your informant to volunteer that information and fill in the blanks in your matrix under a contrast set entitled, "final drive." Then simply indicate whether the category you are thinking of has that attribute and continue answering your informant's questions until he identifies the term you are thinking of. Then start over with another motorcycle in mind.

- *Card Sorting:* If your dimension of contrast has a large number of categories to define, you can write them all on separate cards and ask your informant to sort the cards into piles. Most informants will ask you how to do this. On what basis is he supposed to sort the cards? You reply that he should do it any way he wants. He is the boss. When your informant has grouped all the cards into piles, you can ask him to identify the principle he used to make them. He should reply something like, "These three bikes in this pile have single overhead cams while these have pushrods." This tells you about a valve configuration dimension of contrast. The final product of attributional analysis is a paradigm. Figure 6.6 represents a partial paradigm of kinds of luxo-tourers. A completed paradigm could easily contain 40 or 50 dimensions of contrast.

tourers	cylinders	vibration	luggage capacity	wind protection
GL1500	6	none	most	best
K1200RS	4	buzz at speed	fair	fair
Voyager XII	4	high buzz at speed	good	fair
FLHT	2	most, lower rate	good	fair

Figure 6.6   Partial paradigm of kinds of luxury tourers

Culture or Personal Meaning?

A number of our students have expressed concern over the objectivity of the attributional sorting task. They ask, "Since informants express their own preferences and concerns during this process, doesn't it produce personal, rather than cultural, knowledge and meaning?"

The answer is that of course personal preferences are expressed during the sorting for meaning. For example, GW members prefer the GL1500,

Harley Owners Group (HOG) members prefer the FLHT. Indeed, if every rider who enjoys long-distance riding agreed on a ranking of motorcycles, only one brand would sell.

What is cultural about attributional analysis are the dimensions of contrasts the process yields. Most motorcyclists will agree on the list of dimensions on which they compare or judge the machines. These dimensions are shared categories. Personal knowledge comes into play when informants evaluate this shared information. Most Harley riders like the vibration given off by their machines. Most Honda Gold Wing riders do not. But all of them use "vibration" as a dimension of contrast. It is a shared cultural component of meaning.

Paradigms and the attributes they contain are essential to effective ethnography. The reasons for this and strategies to use them are the topic of chapter 9.

Ethnographic Detail and Cultural Focus

Discovering folk terms, eliciting taxonomic structure, and sorting for attributional meaning are the core tasks of ethnosemantic ethnography. However, there are four additional factors that contribute to successful ethnography: detail, focus, the discovery of adaptive strategies, and the identification of cultural themes. In this chapter, we will discuss the first two activities in the context of questions that often arise after you have completed two or three interviews: "My informant is repeating herself. What do I ask now?" "How do I decide which direction the ethnography should go in?"

Eliciting Ethnographic Detail

As we noted above, it is common after completing about three interviews to, as one of our students put it, "hit the wall." By then you have asked about your informant's average day, identified different kinds of people who participate in the microculture, and elicited descriptions of many activities. You begin to feel that you have "asked it all" and informants seem to think they have told you everything they know. Boredom may set in and informants may lose enthusiasm for the project.

There is no quick fix for this problem but there are several strategies you can use to break the impasse, all of them designed to produce more ethnographic detail and generate more questions.

- *Look carefully at your field notes for kinds of:*

  actions   places   times

  things   feelings   events

  people

  Couple what you learn with different semantic relationships. For example, are there kinds of events, ways to do events, steps in doing events, and parts of events? It is easy to overlook categories that already seem common or partly meaningful but that probably have "inside" significance in the microculture you are learning about. Use the categories you find to create descriptive and structural questions. Additional detail and a sense of movement should result.

- *Look at the dimensions of contrast* you discovered once you have sorted some contrast sets for meaning. Dimensions of contrast often reveal new areas of ethnographic interest you haven't dealt with in previous interviews. For example, if you are interviewing a GW member, he might tell you that *wind protection* is an important dimension of contrast that attributes meaning to *touring bikes*. If you haven't already asked him about it, inquire whether wind is a problem and ask him to describe the effects wind has on riding and riders and what can be done about it.

  If you were to do so, you would discover that wind pressing on a rider's body and helmet is tiring, that it is noisy, making it difficult to hear one's *co-rider* and *radio* over the *intercom*, that it is deafening unless you wear *ear plugs*, and that it overheats riders in summer and causes hypothermia when it is cold. He may add that the ways to control wind involve the use of *fairings*, *windshields*, and *accessories,* such as *wind* and *foot wings*. In short, the discovery of wind protection as an important dimension of contrast in a paradigm leads to a whole area of additional cultural information.

- *Collect stories* because they often reveal information leading to new cultural areas. If your informant is currently participating in her microculture, ask something like (using GW culture as an example), "Tell me, did anything special happen at the last rally you attended?" The general rule, as we have noted before, is to include as much contextual information as possible in your questions to help informant recall. A sample story might look something like this:

  > Well one thing that happened at the Tri-State in Sioux Falls last year was the grand parade was scheduled for 4:30 in the after-

noon—Saturday. So we were told to form up in the park down by
the falls and we got there and all lined up. But we were supposed to
have police escort. So there we were. We had the lead bike and its
trailer all decorated with U.S. and state flags and about 150 motorcycles and everyone is standing around and no police. Finally, people just started giving up and rode away back to the rally site. Then
the police showed up about 5:15 and wondered where everyone
was. They had been scheduled for 5:30. Our district director had
screwed up.

The story yields additional information about rally events
(parades), organizational officers, and hints about what to look like
in a parade. Information like this might lead to more material on
internal conflicts that affect the group and some of the ways people
handle them, a good topic for a final ethnography.

- *Make a site visit* to a cultural scene associated with your informant's
microculture. For example, one student conducted four interviews
with a bus driver, meeting her at a local coffee shop that had a quiet
corner that permitted tape recording. When interview questions
seemed to run out, the driver suggested that the ethnographer ride
the route with her.

The experience yielded all sorts of information that had not been
discussed during the interviews. The trip revealed some of the
driver's strategies to *keep to the schedule.* She (the driver) had ways to
spot transit inspectors who were occasionally sent out to monitor
whether or not she was on schedule. Some passengers who climbed
onto the bus seemed to know the driver. Later interviews disclosed
that the driver knew their names or had nicknames for them. There
were also some difficult bus riders. The student ethnographer could
see firsthand how the driver handled them and then later could ask
her about difficulties she had with riders and strategies she used to
deal with them. Since the student ethnographer already knew
something about bus driver culture from initial interviews, he could
easily spot things he had missed. He also witnessed examples of
driving techniques and social interaction that he could use when he
wrote about the microculture.

- *Use the alternating "descriptive to structural" interviewing strategy.* To
take this approach, start with a general descriptive question and
look for possible taxonomies in the informant's response, noting
them down as the informant talks. Choose a domain from among
the responses and use a structural question to elicit its subcategories. Then pick one of these subcategories and again ask your informant to describe it. You can keep alternating descriptive and

structural questions down a path from general to specific until you run out of detailed levels to explore.

This strategy emerged accidentally years ago when one of the authors (McCurdy) recruited his nine-year-old daughter to serve as an informant for an in-class demonstration interview. He decided to ask her about her fourth-grade culture (she was attending a neighborhood grade school) and began the interview with the usual grand tour question. The exchange looked something like this:

> DWM: Heather, could you describe what you do each day from the time you leave our house to go to school until you get back?
>
> H: Well [this dialogue is an approximation since the original exchange was not recorded], I meet Suzy and then we go to St. Clair and get crossed over Fairview. Then we get crossed again just before we get to school. We play outside until the bell rings. Then we go inside, put stuff in our lockers and have homeroom. We do pledge allegiance, then we have subjects until recess. Then we have more subjects before lunch. Then we line up in lunch line and then we get our lunch and eat it, then go outside to play. Then we have more subjects. Then we go home.

The answer was not very long. Normally, the ethnographer might have asked another descriptive question but because he was trying to illustrate all the kinds of ethnographic questions for the class, he decided to ask a structural question instead. He chose to do so using the informant's general category, *have subjects*.

> DWM: OK Heather, you just mentioned that you have subjects during your day at school. Would you call them subjects when you are talking to Suzy? [*This is a native language check question.*]
>
> H: Yes.
>
> DWM: OK, do you have different subjects?
>
> H: Yes, lots.
>
> DWM: Could you tell me what they are?
>
> H: Well, there's language arts and art, but like we only have art twice a week. [*This is an attribute of art.*] And we have science and there's spelling and math and we have gym.
>
> DWM: Can you think of any others?
>
> H: Ah [*pause*] I guess that's all.
>
> DWM: Well if you do think of any more you can tell me later.

The structural question yielded a nearly complete taxonomy of kinds of *subjects we have,* but instead of asking the informant to sort them for attributes, the instructor again asked a descriptive (mini tour this time) question.

DWM: Now Heather, you said that you have gym? Can you describe what you do when you have gym?

H: Well, our teacher says, "Now it's time for gym" and we have to line up to go to gym and go down there to the basement and we put on shorts and a shirt but the boys go to their own place and do that and then we go out on the floor. And the teacher, Mrs. Murphy [not her real name], says, "OK, now we are going to play a game," and so we play a game and that is all there really is to gym.

Again, the ethnographer switched to a structural question based on this now more specific level of descriptive information.

DWM: OK, so you play games, right? What games do you play?

H: Well [*pause*] we play kick ball and ball tag and trench and musical chairs and baseball when we are outside.

Returning to a descriptive phase, the ethnographer asked:

DWM: You said you play trench. Could you describe how you play trench?

H: Sure. [*The informant, who was quite nervous at first, seemed confident now since she was an authority on trench.*] The teacher says we should choose sides so she picks two kids to choose sides, usually Tommy and John, and they pick the kids for their side and then you like stand on two sides of a line and you have this ball and one side gets to start and it's usually, like it's usually Jason or Carl since they are such good shots, and you get the ball and try to hit someone on the other side and they all run away and try not to be hit. If you get hit you got to go to a special place called the trench but you can get out if someone on your side runs across the line and tags you without getting hit. And you win if you can get all the kids on the other side into the trench on your side.

The interview continued with questions about ways to hit kids with the ball, things kids do to avoid being hit, a list of kids and whether or not you wanted them on your team, how girls and boys played differently, and what the teacher did during the game.

This kind of detailed illustration may seem trivial, but we believe it is essential to useful ethnography. There is information here about how kids deal with a teacher's authority, how they develop ranking among themselves, and the cultural patterns that define the relationships between boys and girls. Combining this kind of information with in-depth interviewing about other school scenes, such as *subjects, recess, lunch,* and *homeroom,* repeated patterns may emerge that suggest the existence of broader cultural themes (see chapter 8 for a discussion of cultural themes) and yield theory about childhood relationships. For example, the information could easily be used to critique teaching methods by revealing how kids react to them. Detailed ethnography yields both ideas for what to write about and detailed examples with which to illustrate them.

• *Interview for backstage culture.* Backstage culture is similar in many ways to the part of cultural knowledge we have called "inside culture." In 1959, sociologist Erving Goffman wrote a book entitled *The Presentation of Self in Everyday Life* that described social interaction as a kind of drama. He viewed people as actors on a social stage where, wearing suitable costumes and surrounded by appropriate props and scenery, they played culturally defined roles. He argued that actors also interacted with each other in a backstage area where they could relax and prepare for their more public stage appearances.

For example, when you eat at a restaurant you take the role of customer, which is the "audience" for servers who wait on you. Servers, however, are members of a microculture with a public face but have detailed backstage cultural knowledge. For servers, you are sitting in a *section.* They most likely have *set up* and *watered* your table before you got there. Your table, itself, may be a *two top, four top,* or *six top.* Your servers probably have several strategies to *get you to tip.* They may have ways of dealing with the kitchen cooks to *get your food up fast.* Most microcultures you are likely to study contain a large amount of backstage culture and it is this intimate cultural knowledge that is usually most interesting and useful to discover.

• *Consciously stay naive.* One of the great advantages ethnographers of foreign societies have is that almost everything they see and hear in the field is new and contrasts with their own culture. The foreign setting enables them to stay naive and to ask questions about everything that happens around them.

This is usually not the case when you do ethnography at home. Informants speak English. They often dress and act in ways you have seen before. It is easy to overlook cultural differences under these conditions because they don't jump out at you, and the problem grows even worse as you learn more about your informant's world. As you get used to the microculture you grow less conscious of its content.

To combat this problem, which is a little like "going native," you need to continue to think of yourself as an outsider. One of the best ways to do this is to consciously (and regularly) ask yourself the question, "If I had to be my informant in one of her social situations, would I know *exactly* how to act?" Another way to view this is to think of yourself as a member-in-training for a position in the microculture. This may require you to be systematic with your informants, bringing them back to more specific material when they skip over details.

For example, imagine that your informant is a stockbroker (this example comes from a 1980 study of the local office of a national brokerage firm) and you have asked him to describe what he does from the time he arrives at the office until he leaves work. To stay naive, you think to yourself, "I need to know exactly how to act like brokers. This means I have to find out everything, from how to dress to what to say and do." The interview might go something like this:

BROKER: Well I arrive at the office before eight and go inside to my office.

INTERVIEWER: Do you call it the office?

BROKER: Yes.

INTERVIEWER: So exactly what would I see when we arrive at the office? How do I know I have arrived there?

BROKER: Well, you go in the Sixth Street door, take the escalator to the skyway level, go right and then right there on your right is a kind of glass wall with a door and it says [X] Company on the door and you go in.

INTERVIEWER: When I go through the door what would I see?

BROKER: There are a bunch of cubicles there where the brokers work and behind them are some offices and that is where I work.

INTERVIEWER: Would I see any people?

BROKER: Yes. At that time of the morning some of the brokers would be there in their cubicles and then there is a receptionist—she sits at a desk on the right—and then the women who take orders sit in a special room on the left.

INTERVIEWER: Do you call them "the women who take orders?"

BROKER: Ah—no, we, well actually we call them the cage ladies because the place they are sitting in is called the cage.

INTERVIEWER: So when you walk in, do you say anything to any of these people?

BROKER: Well, yes, at least I always say hello to Judy, the receptionist. She is young and we say like, "You look tired today. What were you up to last night?" She has a new boyfriend you know.

If you continue to think, "I need to know what everything is exactly and exactly how to act," you would discover that you pick up your *mail* and your *Journal (Wall Street Journal)*, that your mail consists of such things as *confirms, red herrings, offerings,* and invitations to *dog and pony shows,* and that you will do a variety of things in your *office* including *posting the books, prospecting, calling clients, cold calling, lis-*

tening to the squawk box, and *reading mail.* You would continue to ask in detail how to do each of these things. Although you probably would not have the experience to *do* these tasks well yourself, you would have discovered detailed inside cultural knowledge about how to do them.

Focusing the Ethnography

If you have chosen to interview an informant about a relatively broad-based microculture, it won't be long before you discover a wide range of social situations and categories. This can present a problem: should you try to investigate the whole microculture in detail or does the short duration of semester-long research make it impossible to do so? Typically, professional anthropologists will try to elicit material about everything, but even they may have to focus. When one of the authors (Spradley 1970) interviewed tramps living in Seattle, he quickly discovered that there were three major subscenes in the world of tramps: the *jungle* (traveling), *making it* (ways to sleep, drink, and eat) and *the bucket* (jail). He decided to focus his ethnography on jail and the tramps' interaction with law enforcement rather than the other two scenes.

Conducting ethnographic research during a semester-long course poses a greater problem because one semester is not much time. As a result, it is difficult, once you learn to generate detail, to interview about everything. A usual solution is to focus the study by concentrating on one part of the microculture in detail.

Note that *you* have to make the decision about what to focus on. Up to this point your informant has largely controlled the flow of information, although you may have already directed the conversation in particular directions by the questions you chose to ask. There is no way for us to tell you what to focus on. Your decision might depend on what interests you about the microculture, its relationship to an important social problem or to an anthropological theory, or what your informant feels is most important.

Nevertheless, one strategy stands out as most useful: focus on a *subscene* (just as Spradley did) or *social situation* within the microculture. **Subscenes** may be social events that happen in a particular place or activities that shape parts of the informant's culturally defined world. For example, one introductory anthropology student interviewed a hairdresser. The student discovered several parts of the culture that could provide a focus, such as hairdressing products and techniques, dealing with the shop's owner, and keeping abreast of new styles. But she decided instead to look most closely at how hairdressers categorized customers, the challenges customers posed, and the strategies hairdressers used to deal with these challenges. This decision informed the kinds of ethnographic questions she asked during the balance of the research.

Another student chose a subscene within a microculture from the very beginning. She found a boy who was a member of a small-town high school class and interviewed him about what he called "picking up girls." Her study required her to collect some general background information about the informant's high school student-microculture, but focused on the pickup process. To do this, she collected a taxonomy of *kinds of girls* and sorted it for *attributes of girls*. She also learned about such things as how boys should dress, what male physical features the boys thought were attractive to girls, what kinds of cars boys drive to impress girls, what were good places to pick up girls, what were good places to take girls to, and how to talk to girls. The focus helped her choose what directions interviews should take and later proved valuable as a way to organize her final paper.

In this chapter we have looked at ways to increase the depth of your ethnographic study and establish boundaries for your work. In chapter 8, we will look at two ways to analyze and explain the cultural knowledge you have collected.

Cultural Themes and Cultural Adaptation

In previous chapters we have stressed an *informant-generated* model of ethnography. We have represented interviewing as an exchange between an informant, who serves as a teacher, and the ethnographer, who acts as a student. Although the ethnographer/student guides discussions by asking ethnographic questions, the informant/teacher remains the authority on her culture. The result is a body of information based on the informant's language and meanings that reflects the shared cultural content of a social group. But anthropologists often take ethnographic inquiry a step further and, in so doing, introduce more of their own observations into the process. They analyze the cultural knowledge data they have elicited to produce a more general description of cultural values and themes and, ultimately, to explain why the culture appears the way it does. Let's look at these two activities.

Cultural Themes

In 1934, anthropologist Ruth Benedict published *Patterns of Culture*, a book in which she argued that every society's culture was integrated by a central theme that she called its *ethos*. **Ethos**, she argued, permeated every aspect of a society's culture. She used the culture of Hopi Indians living in

77

the American Southwest as an example. She noted that the Hopi way of life was organized around and integrated by what she called an Apollonian ethos, which was characterized by moderation and a measured approach to all aspects of life. The Hopi, she claimed, tended to control their emotions no matter what the circumstances or provocations. Hopi work, play, ritual, religious belief, and worldview all displayed an Apollonian reserve.

If you were to apply the concept of ethos to the study of the microculture you are working on, you should be able to see that a single principle runs through (is displayed by the content of) nearly every taxonomy, paradigm, description, and story that you have collected. Ethos would be part of the culture, hence part of your cultural description. It would be the central theme that tied all the other parts together, a deeper layer of culture on which the more "surface" cultural aspects are built.

Although *Patterns of Culture* was and continues to be widely read, many anthropologists felt that there was little evidence that a *single* ethos organized every culture. They cited examples to show that Benedict had overlooked instances of emotional display and excess among the Hopi and that it was unrealistic to claim that only a single overriding principle organized that society.

In 1945, an anthropologist named Morris Opler introduced the concept of cultural themes to answer this criticism. Instead of a single ethos, Opler argued, there were *several* (but still a limited number of) general recurrent themes that integrated parts of a culture. He defined a ***cultural theme*** as "a postulate or position, declared or implied, and usually controlling behavior or stimulating activity, which is tacitly approved or openly promoted in a society" (1945:198). Like ethos, Opler's themes reflect "deep culture." Opler saw themes as something like core values that a cultural group might or not be consciously aware of and that are expressed in many, but not necessarily all, parts of the culture. They serve as integrating forces that tie cultural components together and guide behavior and interpretation. Opler also noted that themes could conflict with one another in some situations.

Opler used Apache culture to illustrate the nature and application of cultural themes. He argued, for example, that among the Apache, there was a tacit theme that *men are physically, mentally, and morally superior to women*. Opler asserted that themes were "expressed" (displayed) in many parts of the society's culture. For example, women were thought to cause family fights. They were supposed to be more easily tempted sexually and they never assumed leadership roles. The theme tied together many beliefs, social structures, and behaviors expressed by members of the cultural group.

Discovering Themes

We suggest that the identification of cultural themes is an important final step in the ethnographic process, and that toward the end of your study you do a theme-based analysis of the microculture you have been working on. Start by rereading your field notes. Look for recurring similarities that might form a more general theme. For example, if you had been interviewing a GW member, you would discover that members frequently ride together as male-female couples. Furthermore, couples tend to dress alike with matching jackets, pants, and vests. Often they wear the same array of patches and pins on their vests displayed in the same positions. They frequently have their names painted on the rear trunks of their motorcycles and backs of their helmets. They often hold association volunteer positions as a couple (although officially only one of them can do so). There are *couples of the year (COYs)* chosen at the chapter, state, region, and national levels. The Gold Wing motorcycle is preferred by GW members because they believe it carries two people better than any other motorcycle. Almost everywhere you look in this microculture, you will see evidence of a theme that in the GW world it is *desirable and important to participate as a couple*.

The couples theme is *tacit*. Most association members will not tell you that this theme exists. It is simply evident from the association's structure and other parts of the culture. But there are GW themes that are *explicit*, that members consciously insist are important. The theme *concern for safety is essential for GW members* is one of them. The association motto is "Friends for Fun, Safety & Knowledge." There is a *safe miles ridden* vest patch and arrangements for all members to take ERCs (Experienced Rider Courses) if they choose. At every level of the association structure, there are officer volunteers, called *educators*, who promote safety. A cultural attribute of the Gold Wing motorcycle itself is its record of safety. *Group rides* are structured for safety with a *road captain* in front and a *tail* behind. Most association members use CB radios to convey the presence of road hazards to others riding in a group. Again, these are all expressions of the safety cultural theme.

The best way to discover explicit cultural themes is by looking in your notes for them. Often informants will express explicit themes openly, so search for broad value statements.

Another method that works best for the discovery of tacit as well as explicit themes is based on the principle of contrast. To do this, try to compare the microculture you are working on with ones you are at least somewhat familiar with (you can also ask your informant to make this comparison) that appear to resemble it. This may help you isolate dimensions of contrast that turn out to be cultural themes.

Again using the GW as an example, the cultural beliefs of GW and HOG (Harley Owners Group) members reveal important differences that reveal the existence of GW cultural themes. GW members think Harley riders are people who ride to make a nonconformist, slightly outlaw, "statement." They believe that Harley riders purposefully look scruffy, dress in black, and modify their bike's exhaust systems to make them louder as a way to appear "free" and independent, and to rebel against "normal" society. Harley riders, on the other hand, think of GW members as the "mom and pop crowd" who ride "rice burners" (Japanese motorcycles) covered with plastic that aren't true motorcycles and who lack the toughness and dedication of *real* "bikers." The contrast between Harley rebellion and Gold Wing conformity comes through clearly in this comparison.

From the comparison it is possible to identify a GW theme that asserts *it is good for GW members to live by normal North American behavior and ideals.* (Note that themes are stated as positive values in the examples above. We suggest that you represent them this way too.) Once you identify a theme using the comparison technique, you can review your field notes for cultural expressions that illustrate it.

Cultural Strategies

Another way to integrate (and to some extent explain) ethnographic data is to view culture as a set of strategies used to conceptualize and deal with challenges. Challenges take two (although overlapping) forms: ***environmental challenges*** imposed on the members of a microculture by the physical and social contexts in which they operate, and ***goal-related challenges*** (like the themes we have already discussed) that microcultural members impose on themselves. Look at challenges as problems that members of a group try either consciously or unconsciously to meet with culturally shared perceptions and strategies.

Let's use a simple example to illustrate these two kinds of challenges. Many years ago one of the authors (Spradley) required his students to conduct observational ethnography rather than research based on interviews. (See Spradley's 1980 book, *Participant Observation*, for a systematic way to do this.) Students were asked to find one social activity, such as using a Coke machine, riding in an elevator, or greeting each other on a sidewalk, and systematically observe people's behavior. The idea was to have students categorize the behaviors they witnessed and attempt to explain them.

One student decided to observe classmates crossing a street that bisected his college. The street was four lanes wide and the crossing point he chose to observe, because it was in the middle of the block, was not an official and marked pedestrian right-of-way. Students had to cross through vehicle traffic there. They also had to make the journey at least three or four times a day since their dormitories were on one side of the street and classrooms were on the other. After watching students cross the street for several hours and taking copious notes, the observer noticed that there were a series of repetitive "moves" that people used as they made their way to the other side. One he called the "no-look entrance" into the street. Others included the "smooth sidestep" and the "one foot delay step."

Since the observer noticed that different people crossing the street tended to use the same moves, and since they did so day after day, the observer concluded that there was a culture or set of cultural strategies for making the crossing. But what were the challenges the culture was designed to meet? One was obviously an *environmental* challenge. Cars did not give street crossers the right of way. Thus, students had to thread their way through traffic without being run over. So there was a *safety* challenge or problem in this situation.

But by itself, the need to cross the street safely could not explain the style pedestrians used to move across the road. The observer concluded that there was a second challenge involved in the process, one that was a culturally imposed rule that required road crossers to *look cool and unconcerned* as they made the trip. We call the latter rule a *goal-related* challenge that probably expresses a broader theme in this student culture.

To get at challenges (you can also call them problems), we suggest that you make lists of them for various specific elements of the microculture you have studied as part of your data analysis. One way to do this is to look at taxonomies that are about *ways to do things*. For example, if you were studying GW culture, a member might tell you about *steps in getting a Gold Wing up on its center stand*. The implication is that lifting the bike up on its center stand is a challenge. You might also learn there are steps in picking the motorcycle up if it has fallen over. This indicates that it is difficult to pick up the heavy motorcycle when it is lying on its side and that probably the bike does fall over from time to time. Keeping it from doing so is another challenge.

You can also look at any other categories, explanations, and stories in your field notes for clues to the existence of problems. If you have collected enough detail, for example, it is easy to end up with hundreds of challenges faced by GW riders. Finding enough luggage space, having your hair squashed under a helmet (*helmet hair* for women), being seen by cars, riding with contact lenses, wind noise, sore rear ends *(numb butt)*, staying warm, cool, and dry depending on the weather, handling the bike in a parking lot, backing up, group riding, and dozens more challenges regularly confront Gold Wing owners when they ride. As a result, GW culture contains strategies for dealing with all of them. (Note that not all

cultural strategies work very well and some challenges are unsolvable culturally. You are most likely to discover difficult problems if you ask your
informant directly to list them.)

Some challenges are more subtle and general. One way to get at these
is by looking at the themes you have previously discovered. For example,
one GW cultural theme is that *it is good to be involved in association activities.*
This theme leads to a goal-oriented challenge, how to demonstrate that
one is involved in the association. Expressions of the theme often contain
the answer. GW members can demonstrate involvement by showing up at
activities such as weekly *rides,* monthly *get-togethers, rallies, fundraisers, mall
shows, chapter kick-offs,* and *dealer open houses.* They can hold offices in the
organization such as *chapter director, educator, treasurer, Webmaster, phone-tree
coordinator, ride captain, recruiter, greeter,* and *editor.* They can wear a vest
with the association, chapter, and office (held) patches on the back and
their *district, chapter, safe miles,* and *Dairy Queen* patches on the front and
sides. (The Dairy Queen patch is an inside joke. It is said that no *real* GW
member can ride by a Dairy Queen without stopping.) They also can display their *membership pin* and pins with *hangers* indicating how many years
they have been in the GW and how many national and state rallies they
have attended. Indeed, finding a place for all these things on one's vest is
a problem in itself for long-term association members.

You can also look for **structural challenges**, ones that occur because of
the social needs of the group as a whole. Again for the GW, recruiting,
retention, competing for leadership positions, difficulty recruiting for
offices, lack of willingness to work, complainers, resistance to following
the rules, integrating new members, making single people feel welcome,
deciding on joint activities, and coordinating riding together are all structural problems that GW culture is at least partly designed to deal with.

Finally, challenges can arise from the existence of **internal cultural
conflicts** and inconsistencies. An example of this is illustrated by a student's study, conducted nearly thirty years ago, of a state PIRG (Public
Interest Group). The student discovered that a central cultural theme for
the group was *all employees are equal.* The roster of PIRG employees, however, included paid lawyers, lobbyists, fundraisers, researchers, and office
clerical workers. A major problem emerged when clerical workers, citing
the equality theme, asked to be paid the same amount of money as lawyers and lobbyists. We have no information about how the PIRG changed
its culture to manage this challenge, but it was apparently successful since
the organization is still in existence today.

Not all microcultures display internal cultural conflicts such as this
but as we will see in the next chapter, the discovery of structural challenges and internal conflicts is often a key goal of professional applied
anthropologists when they conduct ethnography on organizations.

Writing and Using Ethnography

By the time you read this chapter, your ethnographic fieldwork should be nearly finished. You should have collected a body of detailed field notes, taxonomies, paradigms, and informant quotes. You should have identified some cultural themes and environmental challenges that shape the microculture's categories and their attributes. Now, it is time to take the final step in the research process, writing an ethnography. In this chapter we discuss this process, including questions about cultural representation, the importance of a thesis, some strategies to organize the paper, and ways to use taxonomies, paradigms, informant quotes, cultural themes, and adaptive challenges as you write. We end with a section on the usefulness of ethnography as a research tool and its application by professional anthropologists who work outside of academia.

Writing the Ethnography

Writing the ethnography may look easy at first. If you succeeded in the field you have ample data to report. It should just be a matter of putting it all down on paper. But the presence of abundant data actually creates a problem. As the authors of this book as well as almost every cultural anthropologist who has ever done fieldwork can attest, the prob-

lem is not having too little data, but having too much. What parts of it
should you include? What can or has to be left out? What criteria are you
using to determine what to include or exclude? How can such a wide variety of interrelated material be organized? Over the years we (the authors)
have read thousands of student ethnographies and have discovered that
we like some of them better than others. Our conclusions about why we
liked them inform our comments on writing below. Let's look at some of
the strategies that might help answer these questions and help you write a
better ethnography.

Cultural Representation

Before we discuss these strategies, however, we should consider the
task of *cultural representation* in general. When ethnographers write about
another culture, they act as translators. They are *representing* the culture
they have discovered to an audience with whom they already share a culture. A concern about the translation process is the effect that ethnographers' own cultures and personal experience will have on the way they
portray the cultures they seek to represent. This is an important question
because it concerns the objectivity of the ethnography and, in some ways,
the validity of the whole ethnographic enterprise.

The introduction of ethnographer bias can occur consciously.
Recently, several students have written ethnographies with an interpretive
agenda in mind and imposed it on the data they chose to report. To use a
hypothetical example, imagine that you are interviewing a mortician and
you were convinced from the start of your research that he was taking
advantage of bereaved relatives by overcharging them. To make this point
you organize your paper around this thesis and use selective data or actually distort data to support your viewpoint. We would argue that this is a
clear example of cultural misrepresentation. A thesis should emerge
from, or at least be clearly supported by, the data you have collected.

Misrepresentation can also occur unconsciously, and this is much
more difficult to diagnose. We believe that it is impossible for trained ethnographers to be entirely objective, meaning that they can't altogether
leave their own cultural and personal backgrounds out of their analysis
and writing when they portray others. But we believe that they can check
for and reduce distortion in several ways. First, they can become aware of
the problem and try to identify and be explicit about their own personal
and cultural values and perspectives that might skew their presentation.
Second, they can include information about themselves and the nature of
their research in the ethnographic account so readers can judge their
potential bias and impact on the presentation. Third, they can show their
written ethnography to their informants. This is what one of the authors
(Spradley 1975), along with coauthor Brenda Mann, did with the manu-

script of their book, *The Cocktail Waitress: Woman's Work in a Man's World*. Although a few waitresses suggested minor changes, all were astonished to see how well the authors had "got it right." It is not always possible to show your ethnography to your informant, but we encourage our students to do so whenever they can.

The design features of the ethnosemantic approach also help prevent distortion, since they stress and build in the importance of informant control and authority during interviews. In general, informants are most likely to approve of the ethnographer's account when it describes everyday, mostly explicit cultural knowledge. The more that ethnographers interpret a culture and make their own generalizations about it, the more likely the informant may disagree. If this happens, it is important for ethnographers to understand and try to rectify the disagreement.

Writing and Ethics

In an earlier chapter, we discussed the ethical dimension of ethnographic research. We noted that the primary ethical rule followed by all cultural anthropologists should be the protection of their informants from harm. Application of this rule is also essential when you write ethnography. Written documents make information public; what you write can be read by many others. Recent innovations in communication technology make this a reality for all researchers, but this is particularly true when you are conducting research in your home community (Hopkins 1998). To control for possible informant harm, we feel it is critical to disconnect written ethnographic description from real places and people. Use pseudonyms for your informant and people mentioned by your informant. Also, it is best to alter the names of places, and sometimes even events, you have learned about. Additional signifiers like red hair or glasses should be omitted if they increase the likelihood that your informant might be identified. In some cases, however, your informants may want you to use their real name. If you can anticipate no potential harm to them or other members of the microculture, you can honor that request.

In addition, you must always consider what is and what is not appropriate to report about a culture. Some information may have been given to you in confidence, so that no matter how interesting and helpful for cross-cultural understanding it is, you should still not write about it. In general, you should weigh the ethical appropriateness of everything you write when you represent the lives of other people.

Audience

Before you put anything down on paper, identify the audience you are writing for. One audience might be your instructor. Instructors usually have a definite view of what your ethnographic report should look like and you should follow their expectations when you write. Another audience might be a less clearly defined "academic audience." In this case you might employ an academic style that is relatively formal and impersonal and that often contains more passive constructions, literature citations, and technical terms.

Our advice in this chapter, however, is largely aimed at writing for a more *general public* audience consisting of people who are educated but not specialists in anthropology. This means producing a slightly less formal presentation that permits the use of personal pronouns, contractions, and story quotes. It consists of a more narrative, accessible style.

Choosing a Thesis

We suspect everyone has experienced writing anxiety. All of us have stared at blank pages (or screens), made false starts, put off writing in order to do busy work, and felt frustration, and it is particularly difficult to write when we are not sure what to write about.

Student (and occasionally professional) ethnographers have invented several solutions to the problem. One is the *encyclopedia approach* where authors systematically list and describe everything they have learned about a microculture. The initial difficulty with this solution is length. On several occasions students have turned in 250 pages of description, including taxonomies and discussions about every one of their subcategories. Encyclopedic papers are not only too long, they are usually dull and lack internal coherence. To head them off we limit ethnographic papers to ten pages for students in our introductory cultural anthropology course and 30 in our research course.

Another organizing strategy is the *history of the interviews approach*. In this case the writer recreates an account of the interview series, writing a dialogue of questions and answers.

> I asked my informant to describe a typical dog show and she said: "We always look in Dog World to see where the shows are and depending. . . ." Then I asked . . . then she said. . . . [We have seen dialogue like this go on for pages.]

The history of the interview approach has some advantages. It is a narrative. One can almost write the paper around field notes. Organization is based on the way the interviews were structured. There is a problem, however, with length, since most writers will have more notes than they can publish, and with selection, since one still needs to decide what to include and leave out, because such an approach usually lacks a thesis.

The solution we advocate here is to assert a ***thesis***, then use ethnographic information to illustrate it. Assertions need not be world shaking.

An ethnography about a restaurant cook published in the first edition of this book made the simple assertion that cooks in a particular restaurant possessed cultural knowledge designed to insure their success (Schroedl 1972) with special emphasis on three adaptive problems: using kitchen equipment, knowing how to cook, and making food fast. More recently, Meg Ruthenberg (1990), who wrote an ethnography about firefighters, began the task by looking through her field notes and ethnographic analysis. (Cultural themes and adaptive needs often provide the best clues to an appropriate thesis.) What jumped out at her was how much living in the firehouse resembled family life. She found support for this assertion in many areas of her field notes and by using this supporting material, she had a ready-made way to organize her paper. Material that did not sustain her thesis was included as a setting near the beginning of the paper or left out entirely if it had no relevance.

Parts of a Paper

There are many ways to write and organize an ethnographic paper, and there is not enough room to cover them here. (Indeed, since writing is a creative process, ways to write are seemingly infinite.) But there are some suggestions about writing that we hope will help you along in the process. For example, we prefer papers that *make points up front*. Begin the paper with a "lead" that states the thesis. *Use subheads* (many writers don't, but we think it helps you think better and organize more clearly). Make an assertion to begin the section under the subheading. Begin paragraphs with *topic sentences* (a declarative sentence that asserts something). Develop each assertion with illustrations. We often advise students to *write more about less*.

Beyond these general points, we suggest that you consider following a fairly typical model of paper writing found in many books on the subject. Parts of such a model might look something like the following:

Leads. Start your paper with a short ***lead*** section. A lead should introduce readers to the topic of your paper (basically, the microculture) and the main point (thesis) you are going to make about it. To write a good lead, it is essential to have a clear thesis that (preferably) can be stated in a single, declarative sentence. The thesis should be as specific as possible, but general enough to cover what you want to assert about the microculture. Once you are satisfied with a thesis, introduce it within a more general context. Start the lead with broader statements, and then work down to your thesis.

Take the restaurant cook paper cited above. Schroedl writes the following lead as a way to introduce the topic and his general thesis that the adaptive challenges of restaurant cooking require a special culture.

(Remember as you read this that it was written in 1971. Gender roles and restaurant businesses have changed since then.)

> All mankind must eat to live. There are no exceptions to this rule. But beyond this biological fact, all other aspects of eating are culture-bound. The things people eat, the methods of preparation, and the people who prepare the food all vary from society to society. Generally it is women, not men, who cook the world's food. Even in the United States common phrases like *mother's apple pie* or *home-cooked* indicate that cooking is associated with the female role. But in large restaurants, mother is nowhere to be seen. It is usually a male chef who heads the motley crew of assorted cooks, cook's helpers, pantry girls, and dishwashers [who] prepares the wide variety of delectable dishes customers demand in fancy restaurants. The cooks are well aware of this home-cooking and mother-in-the-kitchen cultural stereotype. As one said about the time he was learning to cook, "the chef walked over to my first attempt at chicken gravy, tasted it, looked up to me and said, 'Just like mother used to make.' He paused for a moment of reflection. 'And she couldn't cook either.'"
>
> It is this cultural scene behind the restaurant kitchen doors which is the focus of this paper. This paper is an inside look at the people whose chosen occupation is cooking, or "slinging slop" as they say in the restaurant business. This study outlines what it means to be a cook and what one has to know in order to survive in the kitchen of a large restaurant. (Schroedl 1972:179)

A second way to generate a lead is to *case in*. Casing in refers to a lead that starts as an outside observer's description of behaviors associated with members of the microculture. The description should contain actions that only make sense once they are decoded using information gained from the microculture. An example of a case in, which uses tramp culture, appears in Spradley and McCurdy's (1980) book, *Anthropology: The Cultural Perspective*. To get to a thesis about the importance of culture as a way to understand behavior, the lead starts with this:

> Imagine that you were to visit the older, deteriorating sections of a city such as Chicago, Seattle, Boston, or Minneapolis. You set out to make some observations one morning about 11 o'clock. A lone man moves slowly along the sidewalk toward you. Everything about him seems to announce to the world that he is down and out. Ill-fitting clothes cover a hollow chest and sagging muscles. The lines in his face, half hidden beneath the shadow of a faded hat, suggest that he is old before his time. His shoes are cracked with age and exposure to the weather. An overcoat, pocket bulging from a half-empty bottle, covers a sports jacket that long ago found its way to a second-hand clothing store. . . . You wonder, "Who is this man and what is he doing?"

The case goes on to describe more sights you might observe—a shabby looking man exiting a blood bank, a man pushing an old baby carriage filled with junk—then, using tramp culture, decodes these sights to demonstrate the thesis that tramps have a culture that they use to adapt to the trials of an urban existence.

Settings. Once you have written a lead, there are at least two sections you can use to set the ethnographic study and its microculture. First, many ethnographers include a section entitled *methods.* This section will recount how they came to do the study, how they recruited their informants and related to them over the course of the interview series, the field methods they used, and anything else about the process that seemed to stand out. Second, it is often useful (we feel it is essential), to incorporate a *cultural setting.* Cultural settings contain an overview of the microculture including its locations, kinds of members, and social situations. This is a good place to use some of the more general (and sometimes less interesting) material you have collected. We have noticed over the years that many students prefer to write about ethnographic foci and supporting detailed ethnographic examples instead of including a setting. The absence of a setting, however, often makes it difficult for readers to place more focused discussions in context.

Body of the Paper. The main body of the paper consists of the points and evidence you use to support the thesis. There is no formula for organizing this evidence except to say that it reflects the cultural data you have collected. One way to organize this part of the paper is to make an *analytical taxonomy.* In early chapters we discussed eliciting *folk taxonomies* that consist of folk terms that are included semantically in the speech of microcultural members. An analytical taxonomy is one you create. For example (using the culture of people who operate railroad switches), you might assert the thesis *railroad switchman culture reflects a major emphasis on the control of time.* To support this thesis, generate an analytical taxonomy of *parts of switcher culture that manage time.* Think about what those parts are, list them, and write about them under their own subheadings.

Sometimes you can use a folk taxonomy to organize the body of your ethnography. To illustrate the thesis *learning how to deal with customers is essential for successful hairdressing,* Pamela Mazza (1990) organized her ethnography around *kinds of customers* (each kind discussed under its own subheading) and how the hairdresser had to deal with each. A paper by Donna Carlson (1972) on hitchhiking in Scotland asserted that hitchhiking culture reflected the need to acquire a ride, insure safety, and reach a particular destination. She discovered that these three requirements were reflected in the taxonomy *steps in hitchhiking* and gave each step its own subheading.

Box 9.1   Organizing Ethnographic Data

Ethnographic writing poses some organizational challenges. Bishop (1999) notes the importance of having ample amounts of both time and space in crafting an ethnography. One of the best ways to identify patterns in your ethnographic data is simply to set aside a block of time in which you immerse yourself in all of your interview and field note material. Managing the abundance of quotes, stories, and charts that you likely generated through your interviews also requires space. Having a place to spread out the array of materials you are trying to organize is helpful. You may find it helpful to do a "pile sort," where you put like items together. Using a *spare* copy of fieldwork material (NOT the original), cut your transcripts into parts that seem relevant to potential themes. Make sure you carefully label the parts, e.g. "interview 1, p. 4," to allow you to find the original source as needed, and sort the material into piles.

We should also note that there are a variety of qualitative data analysis software packages on the market, e.g. Atlas.ti, Nud*ist, and Ethnograph, which are designed to assist you with the task of managing and organizing qualitative data. We have found, however, for the projects of limited scope that our students undertake when first learning ethnographic interviewing that these software packages may be too time consuming to learn to be of use. That said, we think they are important tools for students to be aware of, particularly when applying their ethnographic skills to future larger projects.

Conclusions.   Conclusions often begin by restating the paper's thesis and recounting the kinds of evidence that support it. Then many authors go on to talk about the wider implications of the findings. This can be difficult for ethnographers who are new to anthropology, since "wider implications" often reflect a broader knowledge of anthropological issues. But it may be possible to see how your paper might influence public policy or reflect on the cultural stereotypes of the larger society. If you "cased in" to the paper as a lead, you can also "case out" at the end by returning to the same example and using it to sum up your points.

Using Taxonomies and Paradigms

Students often ask us how to use taxonomies and paradigms. We require our students to include taxonomic charts in their ethnographic reports both to show us that they can do them and to convey large quantities of cultural information in a small space. One thing to remember: you don't have to explain every term in a taxonomy. Since you are working in English, the terms may be partially self-explanatory, enabling readers to follow their meaning. Taxonomies also can often be used to support assertions without explaining every one of their subcategories. For example, when he conducted his ethnographic study of tramps, Spradley

(1970) discovered that they had over 100 places to *flop* (sleep). He could use the whole taxonomy to illustrate the assertion "to survive in the city without being disturbed or arrested or affected by the weather, tramps must know about a large number of flops," adding in parentheses a directive: "For example, see figure 1, taxonomy of kinds of flops."

You can also omit formal taxonomic charts but include taxonomic information in the body of your paper by listing it. For example, if you were writing about GW culture, you could include a formal taxonomic chart of kinds of Gold Wings. If you prefer not to use a chart, simply list the kinds of Gold Wings in a sentence that might look something like this: "GW members have an intimate knowledge of the kinds of *Gold Wings* that have been produced over the years, including *1000s, 1100s, 1200s, 1500s,* and *1800s.* Some of these are also divided into kinds of *models—standards, interstates, aspencades,* and *SEs.*"

Paradigms pose a slightly more difficult problem because they are harder for readers to follow and understand. We still require our students to include some paradigms in their final papers and use them to make points. But, often the attributional information contained in paradigms can be included as part of the ethnographic narrative instead of a paradigm chart. For example, if we are writing about GW members, we might say, "GW members prefer the Gold Wing because it is such a good machine for long distance touring. It carries two people easily, is reliable, has more luggage room than any other motorcycle, and tows trailers easily. It also protects riders from the elements more effectively and carries them in vibration-free comfort." All the points about Gold Wings in this quote are attributes found in the paradigm comparing Gold Wings to other luxury touring motorcycles. Most of the listed attributes can also be used to support assertions about GW cultural themes and adaptive challenges.

Using Quotes

We strongly recommend that you include informant quotes when you write. Quotes work well to illustrate cultural categories, and there is no better way to illustrate cultural strategies, cultural challenges, and cultural themes. There are at least three kinds of informant quotes, however, and we find that one type seems to convey the most ethnographic "power." Let's look at each one.

Opinion Quotes. Informants often state opinions during an interview. Some, such as general opinions about what they know or how interesting their culture is (for example, "There is not really much to working here at the bank," or "I have only worked here for ten years. I really don't know much about it.") can be ignored. But some opinions reflect cultural themes ("We GW members are really concerned about safety.") and these

can be used to support a point about the existence of the theme in an ethnographic report.

Explanation Quotes.   Informants also regularly explain things during
an interview. For example, a GW member might say, "Counter Steering?
Well this is a safer way to steer around corners. Instead of leaning your
bike in the direction you want to go, you counter steer by actually steering
slightly in the opposite direction. Although it doesn't seem right, this
drops the bike into a lean in the direction you want to go and you turn
with more control." You can use quotes such as this to explain a cultural
category, but you can also write the description yourself. Using a quote
lends ethnographic authority to your report, but sometimes you can write
an explanation more clearly than an informant can state it.

Story Quotes.   We pointed out the importance of eliciting stories in
earlier chapters, and we want to again stress their utility here. Stories are
the best way we know of to illustrate points. Stories give an "inside" feel
to your ethnography and can often include contextual information that
you don't have room to include in any other way. We find them especially
useful when you want to illustrate the existence of a cultural challenge. In
his paper on restaurant cooks, Schroedl made the point that it is essential
for cooks to prepare large quantities of food quickly. He used a story
quote told by his informant to make the point.

> Oh, my poached eggs. I found the biggest frigging pot in the whole
> joint. I filled it with water until it was an inch from the top. I thought
> there might be a lot of poached eggs. Down there all by myself, the
> chef had all the confidence in the world in me. Sure, because I had
> worked all the other end but I had never worked the Specials and the
> Specials for the day were the poached eggs on toast or hashed browns.
>   So anyway, the orders start coming in. A poached egg. I walk over,
> the water is, well, the water is warm, well, you know. You just drop
> the egg in there and as the water heats up, the egg will do its thing.
> All of a sudden, I had about twenty-five orders and they wanted to
> pick up and the water wasn't even boiling yet. All I had were these
> lumps in the bottom about THAT round. (Schroedl 1972:180)

The quote continues to describe how the informant called for help and
learned to use a small pan to cook the eggs.

If your informant hasn't told you any stories, or if you make points
about the culture but have no stories that can illustrate them, try contacting your informants again to elicit stories that might help. Note that the
story quoted above is about a mistake that happened because the informant had not yet learned enough about cooking culture to poach eggs
quickly. One of the best ways to illustrate the importance of cultural strategies and cultural challenges is with "screw up" stories like this.

Another issue here is the question about what percentage of an ethnography should consist of informant quotes. We limit our students to about a third of the ethnographic report for quoted material, and most of them use less space than that. If the whole paper consists of informant quotes, it begins to look like your field notes. But instructors have different opinions about this subject and it is wise to find out what the class policy is on quotes before you start to write.

Ethnographic Research and Uses

This ends Part I of this book. We have presented one method, the ethnosemantic approach, as a way to discover cultural knowledge and write an ethnography. We have defined culture as a system of shared knowledge, introduced the concept of microculture, identified ways to find microcultures and informants, described how to use descriptive, structural, and attributional questions, discussed ways to analyze cultural data to identify cultural themes and cultural challenges, and made some suggestions about how to write the final ethnographic report.

Research Abroad

We focused this book on the study of microcultures inside North America. But ethnography is regularly used to elicit the cultural knowledge of people living in non-English-speaking societies, and it is often directed at particular subjects and problems. For example, many of our students go on study-abroad programs where they are required to do research projects. Invariably, they find ethnographic research more difficult to do in the foreign setting. Often it is impossible to tape record what informants say. They must usually work in another language, although learning the language eases the problem of identifying folk terms since almost every word will represent a folk category. They may have to interview several informants, not just one. What most students have been able to do, however, is adapt the ethnosemantic approach, with its emphasis on language, folk categories, taxonomies, and attributes, to different field conditions. Above all, they enter the field with cross-cultural sensitivity and ethnographic experience that allows them to initiate and systematically develop a study on their own. They have had experience troubleshooting problems in building rapport and have strategies to continue the research when they "hit the wall," as described earlier.

Problem-Based Ethnography

Up to now, we have limited our discussion of ethnographic fieldwork to *discovery ethnography*. We asked you to enter the field without a set of particular questions or theories in mind. Your goal was to discover the cultural knowledge shared by members of a microculture and to let conclusions about it emerge from analysis of the data. In the larger realm of social science research, this would be called an inductive (as opposed to a deductive) approach. You may also find that when you describe the ethnosemantic approach that you used here to others, they may respond, "Oh, you're using a grounded theory (or an interpretive) approach."

Although we think that this discovery-based approach is a cornerstone of the discipline of anthropology and makes a valuable contribution to the repertoire of tools available to understand the world, ethnography is frequently problem or theory based. Let's look at some examples of how you might adapt what you have learned here to conduct more focused research to answer specific questions.

There are a number of other ways to elicit cultural information that complement the ethnosemantic approach. ***Participant observation*** is probably the most widely used. As we indicated earlier in the book, participant observation involves "hanging out" with informants, and interacting with them to ask questions, observe actions, and participate in activities. We made the point that observation on its own can lead to the misinterpretation of culture (think of the superficial and perhaps erroneous understanding of culture a tourist might have). However, observation combined with interviewing is a powerful combination that not only lets you observe people, but solicits their ideas about what their behavior means (see DeWalt and DeWalt 2002; Spradley 1980).

Cultural life history or the ***autobiographical method*** (Bertrand 2000) is another useful ethnographic field method. To employ this approach, ethnographers ask individuals to recount their life stories in as much detail as possible. Although this approach may seem personal (or even psychological), individual accounts often reveal the existence of cultural categories and strategies (see Cole and Knowles 2001).

Case studies are a common way to organize and conduct ethnographic research (Stake 1995). Used heavily in educational settings (LeCompte and Preissle 1993), business, and health-related research, this approach is, perhaps, more succinct than the cultural life history. Case studies can be useful when attempting to thoroughly disguise the specific identity of the individuals interviewed (Omidian 2000).

Other ethnographic approaches include the *genealogical method*, which involves asking informants to identify their kin and reveal kinship terms they use to designate them; the use of *photography* and *videography* to record events and to employ as a basis for interviews; and administering *questionnaires* once folk terms and meanings have been gathered so questions make sense to informants (see Bernard 2002). Even with questionnaires, we advocate for the inclusion of at least some open-ended questions to allow the research to obtain unanticipated responses, a continuation of the *discovery* process approach advanced in this book. *Focus groups* or *group interviews* are also an effective way to generate systematic ethnographic data and involve asking a series of open-ended questions with a group of six to twelve people (Krueger 1994).

Finally, we want to stress the practical utility of ethnographic research, a type of *qualitative* research. Most social sciences have relied on *quantitative* methods as they conduct research. Studies are often theory based and data condensed. Most emerged in the past to account for behavior in Western societies. Most assumed a knowledge of the culture of such societies. This kind of research has and continues to yield valuable answers to many questions.

In contrast, the ethnographic approach developed by anthropologists focused on smaller groups and the actors' own view of their actions. When anthropologists conducted research in societies different from their own, they could not assume that they shared enough cultural categories, including language, with their informants to ask intelligent and valid questions. This issue was heightened when working with nonliterate populations. Ethnography then partly emerged as a way to circumvent problems posed by cultural difference. What has surfaced has been a set of strategies to *learn culture.*

While originally conceived to allow primarily European and American anthropologists to learn about societies in Africa, Asia, or Latin America, ethnography has increasingly proven its usefulness in understanding microcultures and everyday life within North American society (see McCurdy 2003; Gupta and Ferguson 1997) and as a basis for employment (see Omohundro 1998). The following are some examples of the application of ethnographic methods experienced by some of the authors included in this volume:

- Byron Thayer (author of the pest control technician paper) was approached by a major computer software company to apply his ethnosemantic skills to understand consumer behavior.
- Jennifer Boehlke used her paper about tattoo artists as a writing sample to obtain a job in an advertising agency.
- Melissa Cowell, who wrote about exotic dancers and is currently a medical student, has used ethnographic methods in the development of public health surveys and in her interactions with patients.
- John Hoch, the author of the paper about the nightclub, uses his ethnographic interviewing skills to lay the groundwork for more quantitative observational studies in special education classrooms and group homes while working on his PhD in Educational Psychology.

These experiences you have from studying a microculture within a complex society will give an introduction to the potential applications of ethnographic research skills. Using ethnography in nontraditional settings and ways, however, remains a dynamic and vibrant growth area. We look forward to watching the emerging generations of ethnographic researchers take the method in new directions.

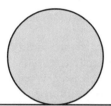

Bibliography

Benedict, Ruth
   1989 *Patterns of Culture*. Boston: Houghton Mifflin. (First published in 1934.)
Bertrand, Didier
   2000 The Autobiographical Method of Investigating the Psychosocial Well-
         ness of Refugees. In *Psychosocial Wellness of Refugees: Issues in Qualitative
         and Quantitative Research* (Frederick L. Ahearn, Jr., ed.) pp. 88–102. New
         York: Berghahn Books.
Bishop, Wendy
   1999 *Ethnographic Writing Research: Writing It Down, Writing It Up and Reading
         It*. Portsmouth, NH: Boynton/Cook.
Carlson, Donna
   1988 Thumbs Out: Ethnography of Hitchhiking. In *The Cultural Experience:
         Ethnography in Complex Society* (James P. Spradley and David W.
         McCurdy, eds.) pp. 137–146. Prospect Heights, IL: Waveland Press.
         (First published in 1972.)
Casagrande, J. B., and K. L. Hale
   1967 Semantic Relations in Papago Folk-Definitions. In *Studies in Southwest-
         ern Ethnolinguistics* (D. Hymes and W. E. Bittle, eds.) pp. 165–196. The
         Hague: Mouton.
Cole, Ardra L., and Gary Knowles
   2001 *Lives in Context: The Art of Life History Research*. Walnut Creek, CA: AltaMira.
DeWalt, Kathleen Musante, and Billie R. DeWalt
   2002 *Participant Observation: A Guide for Fieldworkers*. Walnut Creek, CA: AltaMira.
Frake, Charles
   1962 The Ethnographic Study of Cognitive Systems. In *Anthropology and
         Human Behavior* (T. Gladwin and W. C. Sturtevant, eds.) pp. 72–85.
         Washington, DC: Anthropological Society of Washington.

Goffman, Erving
    1959 *The Presentation of Self in Everyday Life.* Garden City, NY: Doubleday.
Goodenough, Ward H.
    1956 Componential Analysis and the Study of Meaning. *Language* 32:195–216.
Gupta, Akhil, and James Ferguson (eds.)
    1997 *Anthropological Locations. Boundaries and Grounds of a Field Science.* Berke-
        ley: University of California Press.
Hall, Edward T.
    1959 *The Silent Language.* Garden City, NY: Doubleday.
Hopkins, MaryCarol
    1998 Whose Lives, Whose Work? Struggling along the Subject-Colleague
        Continuum. In *Power, Ethics, and Human Rights: Anthropological Studies of
        Refugee Research and Action* (R. M. Krulfeld and J. L. MacDonald, eds.).
        Lanham, MD: Rowman and Littlefield.
Krueger, Richard A.
    1994 *Focus Groups: A Practical Guide for Applied Research, 2nd Edition.* Thousand
        Oaks, CA: Sage.
LeCompte, Margaret D., and Judith Preissle
    1993 *Ethnography and Qualitative Design in Educational Research, 2nd Edition.*
        San Diego: Academic Press.
Mazza, Pamela
    1990 Chameleons: An Ethnography of Salon Hairdresser Culture. Unpub-
        lished course paper, Macalester College.
McCurdy, David W.
    2003 Using Anthropology. In *Conformity and Conflict: Readings in Cultural
        Anthropology* (James P. Spradley and David W. McCurdy, eds.) pp. 386–
        398. Boston: Allyn and Bacon.
Omidian, Patricia
    2000 Qualitative Measures and Refugee Research. In *Psychosocial Wellness of
        Refugees: Issues in Qualitative and Quantitative Research* (Frederick L.
        Ahearn, Jr., ed.) pp. 41–66. New York: Berghahn Books.
Omohundro, John T.
    1998 *Careers in Anthropology.* Mountain View, CA: Mayfield.
Opler, Morris
    1945 Themes as Dynamic Forces in Culture. *American Journal of Sociology*
        53:198–206.
Ruthenberg, Meg
    1990 Home Away from Home: An Ethnography of Firefighters. Unpublished
        course paper, Macalester College.
Schroedl, Alan
    1988 The Dish Ran Away with the Spoon: Ethnography of Kitchen Culture.
        In *The Cultural Experience: Ethnography in Complex Society* (James P. Spra-
        dley and David W. McCurdy, eds.) pp. 177–189. Prospect Heights, IL:
        Waveland Press. (First published in 1972.)
Spradley, James P.
    1970 *You Owe Yourself a Drunk: Adaptive Strategies of Urban Nomads.* Boston:
        Little Brown. (Reissued Prospect Heights, IL: Waveland Press, 2000.)

Spradley, James P. (ed.)
  1972 *Culture and Cognition: Rules, Maps and Plans.* San Francisco: Chandler.
Spradley, James P.
  1980 *Participant Observation.* New York: Holt, Rinehart and Winston.
Spradley, James P., and Brenda J. Mann
  1975 *The Cocktail Waitress: Woman's Work in a Man's World.* New York: Wiley.
Spradley, James P., and David W. McCurdy
  1989 *Anthropology: The Cultural Perspective.* Prospect Heights, IL: Waveland
    Press. (First published in 1980.)
Stake, Robert
  1995 *The Art of Case Study Research.* Thousand Oaks, CA: Sage.
Sturtevant, William C.
  1964 Studies in Ethnoscience. *American Anthropologist* 66(2):99–131.
Tyler, Steven A. (ed.)
  1969 *Cognitive Anthropology: Readings.* New York: Holt, Rinehart and Winston.
Tylor, Edward Burnet
  1968 *Primitive Culture.* New York: Harper Torchbooks, Harper and Row. (First
    published by John Murray, London, 1871.)
Walker, Willard
  1965 Taxonomic Structure and the Pursuit of Meaning. *Southwestern Journal of
    Anthropology* 21:265–275.
Werner, Oswald, and G. Mark Schoepfle
  1986 *Systematic Fieldwork: Foundations of Ethnography and Interviewing.* New-
    bury Park, CA: Sage.

Select Bibliography of Additional Recommended Resources

General Qualitative Research Methods

Bernard, Russell H.
  2002 *Research Methods in Anthropology: Qualitative and Quantitative Approaches,
    3rd Edition.* Walnut Creek, CA: AltaMira Press.
Crane, G. Julia, and Michael V. Angrosino
  1992 *Field Projects in Anthropology: A Student Handbook, 3rd Edition.* Prospect
    Heights, IL: Waveland Press.
Ervin, Alexander M.
  2000 *Applied Anthropology: Tools and Perspectives for Contemporary Practice.* Bos-
    ton, MA: Allyn and Bacon.
Golde, Peggy (ed.)
  1970 *Women in the Field: Anthropological Experiences, 2nd Edition.* Berkeley and
    Los Angeles: University of California Press.
Kutsche, Paul
  1998 *Field Ethnography: A Manual for Doing Cultural Anthropology.* Upper Sad-
    dle River, NJ: Prentice Hall.

LeCompte, Margaret D., and Judith Preissle
　　1993 *Ethnography and Qualitative Design in Educational Research, 2nd Edition.* San Diego: Academic Press.
Lincoln, Yvonna S., and Norman K. Denzin (eds.)
　　2003 *Turning Points in Qualitative Research: Tying Knots in a Handkerchief.* Walnut Creek, CA: AltaMira Press.
Pelto, Pertti J., and Gretel H. Pelto
　　1978 *Anthropological Research: The Structure of Inquiry, 2nd Edition.* Cambridge: Cambridge University Press.
Sanjek, Roger (ed.)
　　1990 *Field Notes: The Makings of Anthropology.* Ithaca and London: Cornell University Press.
Stake, Robert
　　1995 *The Art of Case Study Research.* Thousand Oaks, CA: Sage.

Participant Observation

DeWalt, Kathleen Musante, and Billie R. DeWalt
　　2002 *Participant Observation: A Guide for Fieldworkers.* Walnut Creek, CA: AltaMira Press.
Spradley, James P.
　　1980 *Participant Observation.* New York: Holt, Rinehart and Winston.

Life History

Cole, Ardra L., and Gary Knowles
　　2001 *Lives in Context: The Art of Life History Research.* Walnut Creek, CA: AltaMira Press.

Focus Groups

Krueger, Richard A.
　　1994 *Focus Groups: A Practical Guide for Applied Research, 2nd Edition.* Thousand Oaks, CA: Sage.

Writing Ethnography

Bishop, Wendy
　　1999 *Ethnographic Writing Research: Writing It Down, Writing It Up and Reading It.* Portsmouth, NH: Boynton/Cook.

PART II

STUDENT ETHNOGRAPHIES

We now present ten ethnographies about a variety of microcultures written by students who participated in our semester-long ethnographic interviewing course over the past several years. Since original versions of these papers were much too long to include in The Cultural Experience, *we asked student authors to shorten them in a way that would leave main points and important data intact. The final versions were then edited for publication.*

We encourage you to read some of these papers during the early stages of your ethnographic project. We have found that it is useful for our students to read examples of ethnographic work, especially papers that demonstrate ways to choose microcultures, find informants, and establish rapport. As your fieldwork progresses, these student papers can serve to illustrate the nature of taxonomies and paradigms and strategies for using data and organizing the final paper.

A final note: Several papers that appeared in the first edition of The Cultural Experience *have been reprinted (two of them several times) in other anthologies. The ethnographic research you do as undergraduates can easily be significant and useful.*

Getting the Truth
The Police Detective and the Art of Interviewing

Cole Akeson

Interviewing is vital to most police investigations in the United States. Physical evidence can reveal a great deal about a crime, but hearing the stories of people involved is essential to understanding how and why a crime has occurred. Interviewing victims, witnesses, and suspects can determine whether injuries result from a fall or a push, sexual acts are consensual or forced, or a lawnmower is borrowed or stolen.

However, for police detectives, *getting the truth* in interviews is not always easy. Perpetrators of crimes rarely want to admit what they have done. Witnesses' vested interests may bias their testimony. Alleged crime victims may make false accusations. Ideally, it is the police detective's role to uphold the rights of everyone involved in a case—even suspects—and the best way to defend rights is to seek truthful recollections of events and motives from interviews. To do this, detectives learn the cultural knowledge necessary to follow legal procedures that ideally protect all parties during the investigation of a *case* while also deploying skillful techniques to question and read the verbal and nonverbal language of their interviewees.

TV police shows often contain scenes of suspect interrogations. Although these scenes vary, many contain images of controlling, sometimes

103

angry, and occasionally violent police officers intimidating suspects. Detectives threaten suspects with more severe charges, lie to them about evidence, and frighten them with stories about the abuse they will suffer when they go to jail. But are these images accurate? Perhaps sometimes, but this ethnographic study of police detectives belonging to an upper midwestern city police force indicates that the interrogation process is a much more subtle procedure. (Readers should note that years ago, this police department adopted the practice of recording and videotaping police interviews.) Police detectives believe that subtle interrogation methods emphasizing rapport are often a more successful way to elicit information than the intimidating tactics portrayed in the media. To successfully elicit a suspect's true story, detectives believe it is best to relate empathetically to their suspects, and use a detective-based cultural knowledge of interviewee behavior, especially body language, to gauge the veracity of what they are being told.

The Study

The following is a study of the cultural knowledge that police detectives use to conduct investigative interviews. It is the result of a series of seven interviews of approximately one hour each conducted with a police detective in a northern midwestern state. At times, when my informant was unsure about whether something was cultural knowledge or personal knowledge (i.e., shared by most police detectives or specific to him), he would ask other detectives for verification. I have tried to note all instances where a technique was unique to my informant, and how it might compare with what other police detectives know and do.

I chose to study the microculture of police detectives for a variety of reasons. Many members of my family have been in civil service professions that required them to deal with law enforcement, so I had often been around law enforcement officials but had never been initiated into their culture. Also, I have an interest in social power and the role of government in society, a subject inherent in the role of a police detective. Finally, I was lucky to find my informant, a police detective who was kind enough to teach me about the profession of police detectives and without whom this paper could never have been written.

Preparations and Procedures

Detectives believe that interviews can often be the most powerful evidence in a case. To interview successfully, however, detectives must prepare for an interview, although the degree of preparation depends on the nature of the case and the detective's personal style. In *person crimes* (crimes against a person as opposed to crimes against property), the victim will be interviewed first, followed by any witnesses, and concluding with the suspect. This order occurs because the victim's story, especially when the crime is fresh in the victim's mind, is almost always the most honest version of events. Background information can then be used to detect discrepancies in the suspect's story. The first interview with a suspect is crucial because it is usually the only one that takes place before a suspect has a lawyer, and therefore it is the only time that a suspect and a detective may talk one-on-one.

Among the most significant requirements when preparing for an interview is to follow legal restrictions that detectives call *procedures*. Procedures are put in place to protect interviewees' rights, to avoid circumstances that would lead to falsified stories (e.g., a *coerced confession*, or a confession given because of perceived threat), and to protect the police detective and department from accusations of wrongdoing. Procedures may be generated by officials at various levels of local and state government, but those relating to *open investigations* and the *Miranda* decision are both widespread and vital to the legality of interviews.

Interviewee	In Custody or Out?	Read for Mood?	Read for Lies?	Relate?	Police Image Useful?	Order in Interviews?
Suspect	Either	Yes	Yes	Yes	Sometimes	Third
Witness	Out	Proba-bly not	Not without reason (check connec-tions to suspect and victim)	Probably not neces-sary (less emotion-ally in-volved)	No	Second
Victim	Out	Yes	Not actively	Yes	No	First

Figure 1   Paradigm of interviewees in a person crime

During an *open investigation* (an investigation in which no arrest has been made), the right to question someone is voluntary. A detective can only ask questions until the interviewee *withdraws permission*. In open investigation interviews, the detective is required to make it clear that interviewees are not under arrest, that they are free to go, and that they are not required to tell the detective anything. If the detective deems it necessary to question a person without voluntary consent, he can only do so by placing the suspect under arrest.

By denying a person the right to leave, a detective must *read suspects their rights*, in other words, recite the rights of the incarcerated as required by the Supreme Court ruling in the case of *Miranda vs. Arizona* of 1966. The police detective must make it very clear to suspects that they have the right to remain silent. Detectives cannot coerce or threaten suspects, cannot imply repercussions or ramifications for not cooperating, and cannot make impossible promises. An interview in which the *Miranda* decision was not followed is inadmissible in court. As my informant noted:

> We had an officer get a very nice statement from a guy he'd brought down here . . . except he forgot to warn him about *Miranda* rights. So it can't be used. So I had time to reinterview the guy in jail, and I don't know why, but he decided to talk some more. But obviously, an in-custody arrest like that, you're deprived of your right to leave, you must advise him before you ask specific questions for a criminal investigation of his rights, and advise him so that he clearly understands you're a cop, you're investigating a criminal act for which he may be liable, that he doesn't have to talk to me, that he can have an attorney, if he can't afford one we'll get one for him. And if he can't wait for the attorney . . . then we have to make sure that he understands all those things and knowingly waives his rights . . . before he talks to you in a situation like that.

In this case my informant got lucky. The suspect was willing to talk to him so he was able to get the statement again and rectify the other detective's mistake.

With the capabilities of modern technology, many jurisdictions now require that interviews be documented in a reliable manner to prove that all rules were followed. In the informant's state, interviews are recorded—preferably on video, otherwise on audio—to document the interview for later review as required by law. Requiring the recording of interviews both protects interviewee rights and preserves detective credibility. This documentation proves that proper procedures were followed and may be called before the scrutiny of a judge. It may also explain a growth in the use of more subtle interviewing methods.

Questioning Techniques and Relating to the Suspect

Detectives have developed an elaborate culture of questioning to use in *in-custody* interviews. They try to simultaneously relate to the suspect's point of view, look for verbal and nonverbal cues indicating a suspect's disposition, and guide conversation toward the missing parts of the story. It is here that police detectives are most called upon to represent the interests of the suspect in *getting the truth*. As my informant says to suspects, "I want to be able to put in a report what you thought, what you saw, what you felt, because I've got the other side, and I've got most of the details . . . but what I need you to fill out is why." On one hand, it is the job of the detective to determine if the suspect is, in fact, innocent. On the other hand, good questioning is essential to determine a suspect's intent. It is very important to discover the suspect's point-of-view, as it can provide vital insights for the detective and will open up a new path to *getting the truth*.

Ways to interview	Relate to the suspect/be nonjudgmental
	Let them minimize/justify
	Find a lever
	Lay bait
	Be a regular/nice guy
	Turn on police image

Figure 2   Taxonomy of ways to interview

My informant and the other detectives in his department prefer a straightforward approach when interviewing suspects, meaning using no *traps* to lead suspects into saying things they would not normally say. A straightforward interviewing technique does not mean that the detective is simply asking direct questions. Rather, the detectives try to, as my informant put it, "pick up clues to detect a secondary theme to play off." They try to relate to the suspect, to see things from the suspect's point-of-view, and then lay the bait by "playing off" their knowledge of the suspect's feelings. The following story illustrates this approach:

> Recently a guy alluded to the fact that he was a changed man from before, but she [the victim] kept doing things and he could tell that she wanted the OLD guy, the BAD ASS back. And I went with that. I said, "I know exactly what you mean. Women, they get hot and start yelling, they're expecting it to come back on them, and that's what you did, right?" And he went right along with it. "You bet I did. I gave her the OLD stuff."

In this way, detectives must change their thinking and their mental self-image to that of the suspect's. This requires a great emotional investment on both sides and can be quite taxing. The detective and the suspect, polar opposites and often adversaries, must meet on common ground—simple humanity—so that the knowledge of one's acts may pass to the other.

In the above case, the common ground lies in the simple conversational framework of a man complaining about his wife and another man sympathizing. My informant has "let them minimize, justify, whatever they want to do" to make the suspect comfortable talking about the acts he committed. The detective is nonjudgmental in the conversation, allowing the suspect to talk about his perceived problems and the solutions he devised, nodding and encouraging after each word as though he agrees and understands. The detective receives the confession, and the suspect receives a sympathetic ear.

Accompanying this ability *to relate* is the ability *to find a lever*, to apply pressure and guide the suspect in the direction the detective wants to go, as my informant did by relating to and then using the suspect's feelings about women in this instance. The detective relates to the suspect, and then guides the conversation in the right direction, "whether it's giving them the avenue or shutting off all the avenues that they're trying to take on."

Relating to the suspect is also how detectives attempt to make suspects comfortable, as in the story below:

> This last fellow that I interviewed was a suspect. I noticed that he had lost the end of a finger and a part of another one, and just out of curiosity I asked him how he did that. "It's old scars." He said he was working in a metal fab shop and clipped it in a sheer, and I said, "Yeah, I worked in a metal fab shop and I squished my fingers in the press brake." Break down the image initially that I'm the cop, that I'm the bad guy.

In relating to suspects initially, the detective brings himself down to the level of "just another guy . . . a nice guy." By downplaying the police officer image—actually working to eliminate the influence of their social power—detectives seek to elicit additional details by being liked rather than feared. As my informant said, "We're the guys who gave them the last six speeding tickets. Guys who used to chase them through the woods from the beer party and things like that. . . . I want to remove myself from that."

Although it is often difficult for a detective to assume the persona of a common person, the police persona can be reinstated instantaneously. As my informant said, "I can always turn it on." Often male detectives use their police persona when dealing with young men. Young men around the age of twenty often try "to take control of the conversation, take control of how [the] interview's going." When dealing with suspects who try to assert their authority, the superior social power of detectives becomes an asset rather than a detriment.

Reading Body Language

Detectives believe they are able to relate and *to find the lever* because they know how *to read* people, to watch and listen for behavioral indicators in both body language and verbal language that indicate what a person is thinking. While reading can be applied to witnesses and victims, reading is most useful with suspects. My informant continually emphasized that reading people is a skill derived partially from training and partially from experience, and different people have unique ways of displaying these nonverbal cues. However, he did mention some common signs (see figure 3) and typical responses (see figure 4).

Some indicators occur throughout the interview. For example, holding a very rigid overall demeanor and position at all times indicates that a person is

Kinds of body language	Slight movements	Steady, direct eye contact Breaking and reestablishing eye contact Looking down constantly Gradually looking down Looking straight up, or straight up and left Leaning forward Leaning back Arms crossed Using hands in speech Touching self
	Full body movements	The sigh Defecate Urinate Jumping up, shouting obscenities Telegraphing

Figure 3   Taxonomy of kinds of body language

Slight Movement	Thought Reflected?	Comfort Level with Detective	Appropriate Action for Detective
Eyes steady, direct	Lying	Low	Use background information to counter, or other technique
Eyes changing contact	Truthful	High	Accept and encourage
Eyes looking down constantly	Refusing to speak, participate	Low	Try different technique, detect various secondary themes
Eyes gradually looking down	Wants to tell	Medium	Give opening
Eyes looking up	Preparing to lie	Low-medium	Distract from lie
Leaning forward	Interested, alert	Medium-high	Continue as planned
Leaning back	Relaxed	High	Depends, why is the suspect so comfortable?
Arms crossed	Refusing to speak, participate	Low	Try different technique, test secondary themes
Using hands in speech	Comfortable, normal	High	Continue as planned
Touching self	Preparing to lie	Low-medium	Distract from lie

Figure 4   Paradigm of kinds of slight movements

familiar with police techniques and is seeking to evade reading, as my informant reflected:

> Sometimes they'll telegraph me that they know some of the things that I
> know because they'll take a very specific position or demeanor, and
> they'll try like hell not to change it at all. They'll try to be totally STONE-
> FACED so that I can't do some of the things that I do to read them. To
> me that just tells me you're guilty as hell . . . but it makes it harder, very
> low likelihood of getting a full confession out of somebody that takes that
> kind of a demeanor.

Signs of eye contact also occur throughout the interview. Unwavering,
constant eye contact suggests that suspects are trying to lie, because they
believe that by maintaining steady eye contact they will appear honest. Notic-
ing this nonverbal cue can be useful later if the lie contradicts solid background information. Looking upwards sometimes suggests that suspects are
trying to think of a good lie, and the detective will try to interrupt their train
of thought. Breaking eye contact occasionally and reestablishing it again is
"natural human behavior," and usually signifies a normal conversation that
should be encouraged. If suspects look down for some time, they may be
seeking an opportunity to tell their stories. The detective must make it clear
that suspects will not be judged, but rather that the detective will listen and
try to understand the suspects' side. Looking down at one's shoes throughout
an interview strongly suggests, like the resisting full body pose, that the person is trying to avoid letting anything out, and perhaps different interviewing
methods should be attempted.

Detectives believe that body position can also indicate certain thoughts.
A person leaning forward is probably interested, active, and/or alert, and the
interview relationship is working well. Leaning back is more relaxed, perhaps
signaling that he or she is comfortable. Crossed arms, however, may signify a
refusal to cooperate or let anything out. Accompanying body position are
signs given off from arm movement. For example, "talking with your hands"
is fairly standard for most people and is another good sign, while suspects
who touch themselves with their hands tend to indicate that they are stalling,
being deceptive, or in general thinking of a lie. They should be diverted.

Some suspects will react quite angrily to a high-pressure treatment and will
confront the detective, jumping out of the chair and yelling obscenities. If the
detective can *reinitiate* after that point, it will only be after a "lot of
BULLSHIT," by attempting to start a conversation again on any topic available
and perhaps taking a break from the interview room. Sometimes *reinitiation* is
simply not possible. However, if it is, it will only be achieved by completely
adopting the "nice guy" image in the hopes of relating to the suspect.

The most important body language indicator is, as my informant put it,
"*the sigh.*" In an interview with a suspect, especially a high-pressure interview,
the sigh is the moment when suspects give in. Suspects let out a loud sigh.
The "shoulders drop, usually their neck relaxes and their head doesn't tip

over but it sinks a little." Sometimes—at times when suspects have an especially dire personal story behind their crimes—the sigh is accompanied by defecation or urination. My informant told one story about a pattern sexual offender that strongly illustrates this moment of opening up:

> He was a pattern offender on young children, didn't matter boy or girl. . . .
> He lost total control of his bowel and his urine, and then he told me about
> his uncle . . . about his uncle when HE was a kid . . . and then he went on
> to confess.

When a suspect reaches this point, the detective gives positive reinforcement to the suspect, encouraging the suspect to tell the story. Suspects who reach this point, as described in the example above, are ready to confess.

Conclusion

The police detectives' method of interviewing is one that emphasizes culturally defined techniques they believe develop a positive relationship with an interviewee, and that use that relationship to convey a feeling of understanding and nonjudgment. As suspects become more comfortable with the detective during the process of minimizing and justifying their deeds—both for themselves and for the detective—the detective works to find a lever, a key topic that will cause an admission of guilt, ideally a full confession. To find this lever the detective must learn to read interviewees, to detect not only verbal cues but also nonverbal cues, as hints of hidden thoughts. When a lever is found, the detective lays the bait, hopefully resulting in a confession, or at least taking the detective a step closer towards getting the truth.

Although each case is different and requires adjustments to this template—especially when dealing with confrontational suspects, usually young men—this method has proven highly effective for police detectives. This subtle method of relying heavily on interpretation of human behavior seems much more reliable and realistic than the more aggressive actions of detectives often portrayed in the media.

Juicing Their Way to the Top
Ethnography of a Tattoo Shop

Jennifer Boehlke

I talked to a friend on my cellular phone as he guided me through one of the seediest streets in the city. He had been delayed at *the shop* and was not going to be able to meet me at his house as we had planned. Instead, he invited me to eat take-out food with him at the shop. After passing rows of used furniture stores, fast food restaurants, ethnic grocery markets, and pawnshops, I finally spotted his car parked in front of a tattoo shop with a bright neon sign saying "Damascus." (All names of people, organizations, and places are fictitious.) Inside the shop, I am greeted by a group of about seven men. Some of them are friends whom I originally met in a bar. Most of them are heavily tattooed and bear several body piercings. I am instantly offered a seat at a large round black table located at the front of the shop, where they are eating "authentic" Mexican food, prepared by two "grand-mas" in the store next to the tattoo shop. One friend, Chris, passes me the tamales and apologizes for not having silverware, while another, Adam, is busy creating a makeshift spoon for me out of a Styrofoam cup. Chris is the owner of the store; he does tattoos and body piercings. Adam is Chris's best friend who works at the shop as a body piercer.

As my eyes wander, I notice that the shop is divided into four main sections: the front area contains a round table, a couple of leather sofas, and a display case containing body jewelry, several custom-made knives, and adver-

112

tisements for a local night club. A blocked-off area, which I later learn is the "office," is located to the right of the front area, while the tattoo area—which takes up the majority of the shop—is to the left. The tattoo area contains three tattoo stations and an artist table. Each station has a chair, a power source, a tattoo gun, bright lighting, and a table covered with plastic sandwich bags, a container of Vaseline jelly, and large glass jars holding plastic gloves, tongue depressors, ink caps, and razor blades. I notice that a large red curtain sections off the back right corner of the tattoo area. Adam explains to me that this area is his "Elvis shrine," where most piercings and some "strategically" placed tattoos are given. The walls of the entire shop are covered with giant, colorful paintings that have a "trippy" feel about them.

There is a strong scent of incense mixed with cigarette smoke wafting through the shop. Our dinner is accompanied by the blaring music of Stone Temple Pilots playing on the stereo and the constant hum of the *tattoo gun*. One of the tattooists is working on an Asian woman and her boyfriend. I recognize her boyfriend as one of the waiters who works at a popular downtown restaurant. Some of the guys with whom I am eating get up at various intervals to see how the tattooing is going. "That shit is dope" or "It's looking really good" they would say, as the couple smiles and agrees.

Throughout the meal, the conversation revolves around music, plans for a diner that several of the guys are opening, and general occurrences that took place in the shop that day. Several people had come and gone. One man had stopped in to let the guys know that he had obtained some sawed-off guns for sale. He was a shaggy, older man who seemed incredibly wired and paranoid. The guys simply humored him by listening to his pitch about the latest "weapons" he had to offer and then declared him as "whacked" when he left. Another man covered in heavy gold jewelry stopped by in search of a lost bracelet. The handful of potential customers who wandered in were greeted with a "What can we do for you?" or "What do you have to work with?" followed by "Do you want to look at some tattoo books?" A couple of people settled into the leather couches and perused the tattoo books for about an hour as we ate.

The quick one-hour dinner I had planned at the tattoo shop turned into a four-hour hanging-out adventure. I had seen and interacted with a larger variety of people in one evening than I had during the entire previous month. What caught my attention was the fact that the men who worked at the shop not only made me feel comfortable enough to stay so long, they related to *everyone* who walked through the door with the same charm and ease. A tattoo shop can be very intimidating, but they make it a pleasant place to be. They could relate to a club-owner, a biker, a businessman, a young couple, and even an anthropology student! Adam comments,

> I'm a fucking chameleon to society. I could sit down at a stool at the bar and talk intellectually with a guy in a suit, talk with you about a Cuban writer, or walk out the door and talk to a fucking bum on the corner about drinking whiskey. Any of those formats, I will become a chameleon to that situation because of the fact that I work in a tattoo shop.

I realized that these men were incredibly talented and knowledgeable about dealing with people and that this seemed to be a special feature of tattoo shop culture. The emphasis on social ability interested me and I wanted to learn more about it. I spent the next three months conducting interviews, spending time at the shop, and even getting a tattoo myself in order to understand exactly how this microculture works. I wanted to determine how they manage to attract customers, make them feel comfortable in an atmosphere that is often intimidating and associated with pain, and even encourage them to return for repeated visits.

Chris and Adam worked together as my main informants. They were able to "play off" each other in a way that was extremely effective in the interview process. During the first interview they revealed a "catch term" that expressed how they relate to customers: juicing. Chris explains, "*Juicing* is like going to see what's up, good cop/bad cop, the high-low game, under the table . . . all things that can be included as talking to the customer and getting them to get tattooed."

I soon discover that juicing not only includes ways to get someone to get a tattoo, but also how to make them feel good about doing it and make them want to come back for more. Chris and Adam also informed me of the various concerns or reservations that people have regarding the tattoo process. They highlighted six main issues that seem to be a source of anxiety for their customers: permanence of the tattoo, cost of the tattoo, disease and infection, quality of art, privacy, and pain. This ethnography is an attempt to organize and explain how these men help to overcome several of these concerns through their technique of juicing. What follows is an abbreviated version of the original ethnography in which these concerns and the cultural strategies tattoo artists use to deal with them are addressed.

Things people worry about when getting pierced or tattooed	
	Permanence of the tattoo/piercing
	Cost of service
	Infection of tattoo or piercing
	Quality of art
	Privacy
	Pain of the procedure

Figure 1   Taxonomy of things people worry about when getting pierced or tattooed

The Art of Juicing

The first step in building a relationship with tattoo or body piercing customers is to meet them and to get them to stop by the shop. This is where the technique of juicing is indispensable. Chris and Adam spend a considerable amount of time in bars, putting two variations of juicing to use: the *flirt juice* and the "*we'll take care of you" juice.*

The "we'll take care of you" juice may be performed by either one of the shop employees, friends, or previous customers and may take place anywhere. It consists of catching someone's eye (usually by revealing your own tattoo), talking to them, and then encouraging them to go to the shop by insisting that "we'll take care of you." If it is a friend, they might say, "Tell them I sent you. They'll take care of you."

The flirt juice, a technique used mostly on women, is performed by shop employees. It may be used in a bar or social situation in order to get someone to stop by the shop for the first time, or it may be used in the shop in order to get customers to return. Chris explains how this is done.

> You are having a few drinks, having a good time. You see a good looking female, she's got a navel piercing, she's attractive, you look at yourself and you say, "I'm not an ugly man. I work at the tattoo shop. I could go over and juice her." It's nothing intimate. It's just you walk over, you compliment her, you say, "How are you doing?" Then you flip out a card and say, "By the way, that's a nice navel piercing you have there. You should come down and get some work done by me." That's called the flirt juice, when you use appearance or looks to win the young lady over, or young man, whatever. What it comes down to is you can be a little extra nice to them and they think they are special and they'll come down (to the shop) to see you.

One problem that my informants have is that they may not remember someone whom they juiced while they were drinking at a bar. "They'll come down to the shop and be like 'don't you remember me?' and we'll be like, 'NO, but don't feel bad.' But at the same time, it worked out pretty well because they came down, they were *juiced.*"

Flirting with customers has also led to another phenomenon—groupies. Adam and Chris explained: "For a certain period of time you'll get a pack of young girls who are kind of 'in lust' with us. It is kind of funny because they will come in and they will bring all their friends. They will be like, 'Come see who works here, they are really nice (or they're really cute).'"

Once the customers are lured into the shop, the next step is convincing them to get a tattoo. This requires the tattoo artist or body-piercer to be able to offer plenty of reassurance regarding the customer's decision. They have to be able to counteract years of negative connotations regarding tattoos and pacify the customer's fear of applying a permanent mark on their body.

Show Me the Money!

Once a customer has decided to get a tattoo or piercing, the next step is arranging payment. Tattoo shops have a general up-front payment policy.

This is due to the fact that customers have been known to run off without paying, or simply do not have enough money on them.

Since many customers are concerned about the expense of having a tattoo applied, the shop has developed many juicing techniques that allow them to charge the most money possible, while making the customers feel as though they got a good deal. These *juice mechanisms* include the *high-low game, good cop/bad cop, under-the-table, add-on juice, come back juice,* and *"What do you have to work with?" juice.*

The classic juice mechanism is the *"What do you have to work with?" juice.* I saw this used many times during my first visit to the tattoo shop. It involves one of the men in the shop asking the customer, "What are you looking to spend today?" or "What are you working with today?" as soon as they walk through the door. This allows the tattoo artist or body piercer to determine how much money the customers have with them that tattooists can get them to spend. They try to make their service affordable while making a profit at the same time.

However, since tattoo customers have become quite adept at bargaining for a good price, my informants don't always rely on what the customer claims he or she is willing to spend. They often try to determine how much people will spend before they even walk through the door. All of the artists at the shop play a game called the *"who's coming and what are they coming for?" game.* Since the shop has big windows, the artists often see the customers as they approach the door and they try to guess what the customers want and how much they can get them to spend.

> One of us will be like, "No, they're coming in for a tongue piercing." "No way man, that girl is getting a tat on her arm, that's why her mom is with, you know." So we have this guessing game of what is going on and what they are going to get. To be honest with you . . . we are usually right.

Once the tattoo artists have determined how much they can probably get the customer to spend, they agree on a price. This may involve further juicing mechanisms such as the high-low game, good cop/bad cop, or under-the-table.

> We have good cop/bad cop. What that [consists of] is one of the people will be the good cop, which is the person who is going to do the tattoo and, the other, like myself, would be the bad cop and he [the good cop] would be like, "Well, I could probably do it for $200," and then [I] would be like, "No, no, no, you have to do it for fucking $300, $200 is way too low!" And then [we] would compromise with like $250. So I take the bad rap. The [artist performing the tattoo] takes the good rap, but the customer is still getting a good deal. It's just like used car salesman shit. Sometimes people get more than their value, sometimes they get less than their value. It just depends on certain circumstances.

Good cop/bad cop and the high-low game both require the participation of two artists. High-low game is very similar to good cop/bad cop. The main difference that separates the two is that *good cop/bad cop* requires "one person to be the dick and the other person to be the good guy, and the *high-low* is simply a price game."

Juice Mechanism	No. of Workers Needed	Where Mostly Used	Purpose	Unique Features	Phrases Used
High-low game	2	The shop	Charge more	A price game	1. "Well, I could probably do it for $200." 2. "No, no, no you have to do it for fucking $300, $200 is way too low." (Compromise for $250.)
Good cop/bad cop	2	The shop	Charge more	One person is a dick, the other is a nice guy	—
Under-the-table	1	The shop	Exchange "tax-free" services	Service is not recorded for tax purposes	"Oh, you're a painter, we need our walls painted. . . . Oh cool, you want a tattoo?"
Add-on juice	1	The shop	Get customer to come back/apply bigger, more expensive tattoo	—	"Well God, you know since you're already here and stuff, why don't we go ahead and touch up this one; it's small and you could just tip me like $20."
Come-back juice	1	The shop	Get customer to come back	—	"God, that's a really nice tattoo. I know you don't have the money right now, but you should think about getting roses around it, cause it would look really good."
"We'll take care of you" juice	1	Bars	Get customer into the shop	May be done by friends of people who work at the shop	"Hey, go to this shop . . . tell them I sent you, and they'll take care of you."
"What do you have to work with?" juice	1	The shop	Charge the most possible	Called "the classic" juice	"So, what do you have to work with today?"/ "How much are you looking to spend?"
During tattoo juice	1–2	The shop	Make customer feel good/come back	Helps reduce pain of the tattoo	"That shit is dope."/"That's clean, very clean."
Flirt juice	1	Bars and the shop	Get customer into shop/come back	Used mostly on women and leads to having "groupies"	"How are you doing?" (flip out a card) "By the way, that's a nice navel piercing you have there, you should come down and get some work by me."

Figure 2 Paradigm of juicing mechanisms

Permanence of Tattoo

While body piercing seems to be a fairly recent phenomenon in the U.S., tattoos have been a source of controversy for many years. People bearing tattoos have long been identified as "freaks" by mainstream society. They have been associated with rebels, bikers, and broken hearts. Even as tattoos are becoming increasingly mainstream and fashionable, stereotypes are difficult to overcome. Strong negative associations that often surround tattoos are especially intimidating for a potential tattoo customer considering the fact that they are permanent. People who get a tattoo are often making a statement about themselves that will be carried for the rest of their life. Of course, one may opt to have a tattoo removed surgically by laser, but this is an extremely expensive procedure that is financially feasible for very few people and leaves scars. Therefore, the permanence of a tattoo is a large source of anxiety for many people. Chris noted, "People are scared. It's a scary thing for one to put something on your body for the rest of your life. It's scary [deciding] where you're going to put it, it's scary [wondering] how it's going to be done."

There is also a great deal of pressure placed on the tattooist due to the permanent nature of their job.

> It's a fucking weird job. You wake up and you apply something permanent on someone's body for the rest of their life. You're not selling them a bottle of beer, or you're not giving them a fucking omelet on a platter. You're selling them something that is going to be on them forever. It's a hard thing to do and you have to be convincing. Not that you are trying to convince them into something that they don't want to do, you just have to be reassuring. Working in that kind of environment is more psychological than it is anything else.

Since getting a tattoo or body piercing is often seen as making a permanent statement about oneself, the artists want to make sure that customers get exactly what they want. In order to help customers choose what kind of statement they would like to make about themselves, the shop has a large reference library of books.

> Over the two and a half years that we have been open, we went and found all the different topics of things that people are generally really into, as far as tattoos go. We have books on human anatomy, pose books which have thousands of different figure poses, cartoon books, horse books, lettering books, Japanese and Chinese character books, dragon books. It's an essential tool in tattooing. You've got to have reference material.

The shop also has portfolios of piercings and tattoos that they have done on previous customers. These artists are especially talented at creating the perfect tattoo for each individual because they specialize in *custom work*. Custom work is anything that is uniquely tailored to the taste of each customer, not simply something copied out of a book.

> We do mainly custom work, so what we really promote at the shop is
> totally getting people in there, and when they do walk through the door,
> preferably drawing something out of their imagination. It's not like a lot
> of places where you just walk in and pick something off the wall.

Custom work is also a term that may be applied to piercings. This would
include anything that is not the "norm."

One final way that my informants may pacify a customer's concern
regarding the permanence of a tattoo is through a version of the flirt juice.
They might say to a black woman, "You have a really nice complexion, a
gold tattoo would really compliment your skin tone." When customers are
reassured that a tattoo would look good on them, they are not as concerned
about its permanence.

When people have decided to make a permanent alteration on their
bodies and they are paying a substantial amount of money to have it done,
quality of art becomes a major concern. This is not an occupation that
allows room for mistakes. My informants made it very clear that their job is
mostly "psychological."

> It's an easy job as far as time is concerned and being physical about it, but
> it is a very mental job, you can't forget anything, you DON'T fuck up.
> You don't poke somebody through their tongue and say "OOPS!" . . .
> they don't want to hear it, you don't have time to fuck up . . . so that is the
> biggest thing on your mind, you want to get them in there, make them
> feel comfortable, and get them out.

The artists reassure customers that they will receive a high-quality service by ensuring them that they are licensed tattoo artists and body piercers,
that they are knowledgeable about their job and human anatomy, and that
they have had many satisfied customers. They may also use the *during tattoo/
piercing juice* to make the customer feel good about the art.

Although my informants convinced me of their ability to offer quality art
to their customers, we all know that no one is perfect. So the question arises,
"What happens if they do make a mistake?" This is where the during tattoo
juice comes into play. The *during tattoo juice* consists of one of the guys in the
shop walking over to someone else's tattoo station while the artist is working
on a customer and commenting on how good the tattoo looks. I noticed this
technique during the first evening I spent in the shop. While a couple was
getting tattooed, my friends would get up from eating and say "Hey, that
looks really good," or "That shit is tight!" The couple was being juiced.
Adam explained how his friends juiced him when he got an eagle tattooed
on his chest.

> Last night I got tattooed on my chest, and my first question when I
> opened my eyes—cause I was like trying to relax because of the pain fac-
> tor—I open my eyes to the guys standing above me and I say, "Does it
> look tight?" and they looked at me and they's like, "That shit is dope,"
> which means they are juicing me, making me feel better about getting a

tattoo which you can do to customers as well. You like walk over to another artist's station and be like, "Hey, that tattoo looks really good," and the customer is like, "Yeah, you're right." Or we'll say, "That's clean, very clean." Clean is a good juice. It means not crispy or flaky.

The during tattoo juice can be a helpful way to cover up mistakes or flaws in a tattoo that is being given. The artists may compliment each other in front of a customer even if they don't especially like the tattoo. They may also help to reassure customers. For example, if a tattoo is a bit crooked and the customer notices, the other artists may say, "It gives it character" or "I think it looks better that way." They are using *juicing mechanisms* to cover up any minor flaws.

Conclusion

From the interviews and careful observation it became clear that tattoo artists and body piercers have to deal with a plethora of customer concerns on a daily basis. My informants highlighted six main issues that seem to be a source of anxiety for customers: permanence of the tattoo, cost of the tattoo or piercing, transmission of disease or infection, quality of art, privacy, and pain. They proved to be extremely adept at pacifying these concerns through techniques of *juicing,* creating a clean and comfortable environment, and by simply being knowledgeable about their job. It was also obvious that Chris and Adam have learned to be "chameleons." They can relate to just about anybody: a biker, a businessman, a stripper, a club-owner, a bum on the street, and even an anthropology student. Good communication and people skills are talents that will allow them to be successful wherever they go in life. Their techniques of juicing may also be applied to a wide variety of sales jobs.

The bottom line is this: people like to be comfortable. Whether they are having their hair cut, eating at a restaurant, buying a house, or piercing their tongue, they want to be relaxed and assured that they are making the right decision.

No Money, No Honey
An Ethnography of Exotic Dancers

Melissa Cowell

You Do What?

In high school, my friend Shadow (all names of people and places in this paper are fictitious) covered up her body as much as possible, even going so far as to swim in a t-shirt and jeans. She claimed to have picked up the habit at work because she believed clothes protected her skin from the dangerous chemicals she used there. I thought instead that she was simply overmodest. A few years later, we went swimming again and this time Shadow did not even wear a conventional swimsuit, opting, instead, to enter the water in skimpy designer underwear. Clearly something had changed her during the intervening years. After a little probing, I learned that Shadow's transformation had to do with her new job as an exotic dancer. I was curious about her new occupation and successfully recruited her to be an informant for an ethnographic interviewing class that I was taking at the time.

During the ethnographic research, I found that many of my assumptions about life as an exotic dancer were inaccurate. Because exotic dancing challenges societal norms of acceptability, it is true that dancers are subjected to more abuse and less protection from social ostracism than most working people. I discovered, however, that from a dancer's point of view, exotic dancing

121

is much like other forms of employment, simply an economically competitive occupation, although one that presents some special challenges. To succeed at dancing, I learned, dancers must acquire a cultural knowledge used to encourage customers to tip, to handle unwanted sexual advances, and to manage other negative features of the job. They also manage the stigma associated with dancing by expressing a sense of control over their patrons. Above all, acting confident is key to achieving these goals.

Methodology

My first interview with Shadow went fine, but I soon learned that asking a childhood friend ethnographic questions about a sensitive topic such as exotic dancing could become difficult. Shadow soon reached her limits and introduced me to her friend and coworker, Jasmine, as a substitute informant. According to Shadow, Jasmine "gets caught up a lot more in the interesting parts" of dancing, aspects that Shadow avoided talking about.

Because Shadow and Jasmine lived and worked many miles from my home, I conducted all the interviews for this ethnography by telephone. I believe this had two effects on the ethnographic project. First, I wasn't able to visit Club X, the bar in the city of Gotham where Jasmine and Shadow worked most often over the course of our interviews, nor have I seen either informant dance. I felt these were drawbacks given the physical nature of the occupation. More importantly, I could not observe Jasmine's facial expressions or gestures during the interviews and missed whatever information actually seeing her could have offered. On the other hand, the anonymity of telephone conversations with a stranger may have given Jasmine freedom to express things she otherwise might have hidden. The phone certainly disguised some of my own discomfort with aspects of exotic dancing. Because I do not have firsthand knowledge of exotic dancing, I have based my portrayal wholly on Shadow's and Jasmine's accounts.

Working the Floor

Both Shadow and Jasmine work at Club X, one of scores of Gotham bars that serve alcohol and entertainment to a primarily working-class male clientele. At Club X, dancers, called *girls* in this scene, dance on two *stages* in the *main room*. The *main stage* is biggest and features a pole stretching from ceiling to stage. The *back stage* is smaller and lacks a pole. Both stages are raised off the floor and are ringed by a counter, the *rack*, at which customers sit. The bathroom and *dressing room*, dancers' exclusive domains, make up the backstage area and are separate from the main room. If you were to walk into Club X, you would probably see a *bouncer* near the door or on the *floor* (the area between the stages and the bar) checking customer IDs or subduing agitated patrons (and sometimes dancers). Bouncers also play music when the bar is mostly empty. The *DJ* occupies a table next to the main stage and plays music during busier hours. *Bartenders* work at the bar that lines the back wall, and *cocktail waitresses* who work on the floor serve customers drinks. Besides their more traditional roles, bar staff also assist the dancers, scheduling them, letting them leave, rescuing them from unruly customers, and giving them information (*tips*) about what customers like (see figure 1).

Dancers, although not exactly "hired" by bars or clubs, are added to a roster of girls scheduled to dance on a regular basis. Their relationship with the bar and its staff is based on reciprocity. The bar provides a setting in which girls can dance and attract tips, and bar staff members facilitate that process. DJs encourage tipping between songs, saying things like:

> Come on, guys, get up to the rack. You've got what the girls want. It's in your pants and six inches long. Or rather, in your wallet. That's right, those dead presidents. These girls are necrophiliacs. Remember to tip these ladies, gentlemen, because this is pay-per-view. No money, no honey. No cash, no gash.

The majority of girls are minors who are legally only allowed in the bar when dancing. Because of this they often rely on cocktail waitresses for useful information about the customers, such as "that customer just broke a bill," or to pass along messages, "that customer wants a table dance." Being friends with bartenders and bouncers is even more helpful because they can allow girls, who are minors and not legally allowed to be in the bar around liquor, to stay in the bar

Bar Staff	Amount to Tip Out	Gender	Dancers Have a Favorite?	How They Help Dancers
Bartenders	Part of 10% of dancer's earnings	Male and female	Yes	Schedule them, let them get away with stuff, let them leave, give them tips on customers, rescue them
Bouncers	Part of 10% of dancer's earnings	Male	Yes	Rescue them
Cocktail waitresses	Part of 10% of dancer's earnings	Female	Not necessarily	Give them tips on customers, make change for lots of ones, bring drinks
DJs	$5 per shift	Male	Yes	Try to get customers to tip

Figure 1   Paradigm of bar staff's relationships to dancers

between sets. One of the reasons that bartenders and bouncers do so is that the girls bring in the customers. Jasmine noted, "I have people that come in there just to see me. I bring clientele into the bar. There was one guy, when I quit dancing [at a particular bar], my friend told me he was in there looking for me every day for a week." Dancers also *tip out*, or share their earnings with bar staff.

Owners, and especially bartenders, can threaten to *kick a dancer out* (fire her or drop her from the roster) if she is late to work, misses work, or refuses to dance. At Club X, however, a shortage of girls available for some shifts means that bar owners are reluctant to fire anyone for those reasons. Jasmine related an example:

> So the bartender goes, "What are you doing here? You're off the list. You cannot be in this bar." And I go, "You can't tell me I can't be in here." She's like, "Well, I can tell whoever I want that they can't be in this bar because it's my bar. I can refuse the right to serve anyone." And I'm like, "I'm not asking for service. All I'm asking for is that I can get my stuff." So I get pretty pissed off and heated and finally I just got my stuff. And . . . I ended up working in this other bar in North Gotham. I thought I was fired but I talked to my friend who talked to the lady that does the booking and she said, "What? She's not fired." I said, "Of course I'm not fired. I'm one of the few girls that she books there that actually has teeth. And I also have customers."

Although dancers depend on the bar for the opportunity to work, the process of earning money is up to the girls themselves, with a little help from their peers. Initially, girls are scheduled with a *house mom*, a more experienced dancer who will explain and demonstrate such information as how to "bend over properly," *work the pole*, project a certain image, and the local laws applicable to exotic dancing. Dancers also learn new *tricks* by watching more experienced dancers:

> One [trick] that you'll see a lot of people try to figure out how to do is you grab the pole, pull yourself up and sort of do the full splits while you're hanging there. A lot of people will learn it from watching, or from someone who's been doing it for a long time.

However, both Jasmine and Shadow asserted that "pretty much you learn everything on your own."

Dancers develop their own style from experience, primarily from what they find to be profitable. For example, as one said, "You'll notice that some [of the customers] will just stare the whole time at your crotch, and if they're giving you money, you show them your crotch."

My informant's house mom offered a piece of advice that expresses a part of conventional wisdom among dancers:

> You need to remember that ultimately you are always in power and these people are just wallets. The sweeter you are, and the more you can talk to them, and the more you can comply with their fantasies, the more money you're going to get.

This statement summarizes how many dancers look at and justify themselves in relation to their job and their customers. They view dancing as a straightforward service provided in exchange for customers' tips, one with a clearly defined approach stressing that they, the dancers, "comply with their [customers'] fantasies" to gain the most financially lucrative outcome. To deal with customers who choose not to tip, girls use other tactics to ensure a fair exchange.

Fantasy and Judging the Crowd

One way to please customers and increase tips is to create a fantasy persona that is sexually exciting to customers. Many dancers believe that their customers prefer one of two general fantasy roles: the *naive girl* or the *confident woman*. For example:

> I have certain outfits that have become kind of popular. Like my little schoolgirl outfit. It's a super, super short little plaid miniskirt that my butt—the bottom of my butt—basically hangs out of, and then white cotton panties and a little girl t-shirt and knee socks, and then my heels. And men usually request me to wear the skirt pretty often. "Wear your Catholic schoolgirl skirt! I love the Catholic schoolgirl skirt!" Or knee socks. Men love knee socks. I don't know why.

There are other strategies that dancers use to enhance monetary success. While they wait for their set, dancers have the opportunity to scan the crowd and judge which customers are in the mood to tip. Second, girls who are allowed to be in the bar can talk to customers, greeting their *regulars* (customers they know), recruit customers to the rack for their set, or sell *table dances* (personal dances performed at tables instead of on stage). The first tactic often proves rewarding:

> Some people you can pick out because they have "stupid" or "sucker" written across their foreheads. And I've caught those people before. One guy I got a hundred bucks out of in table dances because he wanted to start crying to me, to tell me about how his wife was dying. I realize how it sounds, but at the same time, why was he in a titty bar? Why wasn't he in the hospital visiting his wife? And I told him that and he started bawling and gave me twenty bucks.

The majority of a dancer's income is made from dancing on stage. When a girl's *set* is about to begin, the DJ will announce her, cuing her to get on stage. Jasmine summarizes what dancers ideally do during a set:

> [If] you're dancing a three-song set, first of all, you dance around, go around to each of your customers, flash them a little bit of this, flash them a little bit of that, and . . . ultimately, what you want is . . . each customer at your stage to put up at least—at least—a buck. And the second song, the ones that are tipping, you go back to them and dance for them,

but the ones that aren't tipping, you don't pay attention to. And then you take off your top or bottom depending on what you're in the mood to do. Last song, ultimately, you get fully nude.

How a dancer spends the rest of the set depends on what, with time, experience, and knowledge of the customers, has been successful at generating tips: *pole work, floor work,* meaning "when you're . . . crawling around the floor like doing the splits or pulling one leg up by your head," and continuing to talk to customers, "because a lot of times they'll want to stop you and ask you your name, and they just sort of comment on whatever." (See figure 2, taxonomy of things a dancer can do while on stage.)

A dancer will also watch customers in order to read what they want in return for tips:

> Some people want more attention. Some people don't. Some people express that verbally. Some people express that by looking away from you when you're dancing for them and they have more money up than everybody else. Or maybe they were just drunk and put up the wrong bill. My friend once ended up getting a hundred dollar bill. She said she tried to give it back to [the customer] but he was all, "Fuck you, bitch." We were all, "Ha ha, who got the last laugh, buddy? Who's got the hundred dollar bill?"

Dancers pick up money after their set or between songs, tucking it away on stage, with clothes or in a purse. If they are worried about the customer taking the tip back, however, they will knock the money off the rack onto the stage. According to Jasmine, certain tactics used to pick up money can earn you more:

> Sometimes I'll [pick up a tip] by sitting on it, 'cause my butt's sweaty and it'll stick to it. I don't do that one pretty often because I think it's tacky, but they think it's funny. It makes me look like an airhead. But I'm like, "Ha ha." Little did they know that they're the stupid ones. They keep putting more money up there because I'll sit on it.

Things a dancer can do while on stage	Strip	
	Dance	Do floor work Do pole work
	Talk to customers	
	Pick up tips	
	React to abusive customers	Insult them in a low voice Scream at them Kick drinks over Kick or hit them
	Do specialty shows	Do fire shows Do chocolate and cherry shows Pretend to shower

Figure 2   Taxonomy of things a dancer can do while on stage

Knowing and Setting the Limits

What a dancer does on the stage and for customers is determined, to a certain extent, by the law. However, personal principles, and especially a dancer's sense of fairness and self-worth, are often more important. For example, while nudity is legal and expected in Gotham, Jasmine rarely gets fully nude without sufficient compensation, "because it's not worth ten or fifteen dollars for someone to see me fully nude." Principles become significant when the others in the club test the boundaries of the law and of common courtesy. In the end, dancers must strike a delicate balance with their actions to maintain personal dignity without putting their economic relationship with customers and the club in jeopardy.

Customers often fail to live up to their role at the club. Most often, they do this by failing to tip. DJs encourage tipping, but it is usually up to the dancers to reinforce the idea that customers must tip. Dancers tend to ignore nontipping customers, turning their back so that, according to Shadow, "if he sees anything, it's by accident." In a bad mood, dancers will go so far as to knock a customer's drink over, kick a customer, or throw small tips (usually change) back in their faces. They will also leave the stage, or, as Jasmine implies above, refuse to strip.

> Shadow was dancing before me. She came into the dressing room after her second song, threw two dollars down and said, "Fuck this. You go out there and dance." Well, by the time I get out there, there's five customers out there. Halfway through my second song I had a buck. Usually, when I have a little bit of money out there I'll take off my skirt because it's not very easy to move around in. But I'm like, "No way! Uh-uh. I'm not taking anything off for these guys." They glared at me and I was like, "Well, what do you expect for a buck?"

Customers have been known to verbally or physically abuse the dancers, or to solicit them for sex. To a certain extent, dancers expect to receive some comments or gestures that would generally be considered inappropriate.

> Part of a pretty typical day for me is getting a lot of crude comments, old men flicking their tongues at you, [saying], "Mmmmm, baby, I bet that tastes sweet." You know, on the street, I'd have a downright fistfight, but at my job, I've got to tolerate that. That's part of what I agreed to by becoming a dancer.

Despite the fact that both customers touching dancers and prostitution are illegal, it is not uncommon for patrons to ask for things like *blow jobs, hand jobs,* or *private parties,* in which girls will dance and strip in someone's home and are then usually asked to perform sexual favors. Although my informants do not know (or will not say) how common prostitution is among other dancers, they have both been solicited and both repeat stories, like dancers' folklore, of things they have heard customers requesting:

One guy paid this girl quite a few hundred dollars to go to Hawaii with him, to stay in a hotel. For that week, he beat the living crap out of her. She had to have reconstructive surgery. And he paid for her surgery.

Defense

One expectation shared by the bar staff is to protect dancers from abusive customers. Bouncers make sure dancers are not being mistreated and escort offensive customers out of the club. Jasmine's favorite bartender even jumped over the bar to "rescue" her on one occasion. Unfortunately, club and bar staff members are not consistent allies for dancers. Some bar owners have even been known to encourage dancers' *extracurricular activities,* meaning prostitution. Bartenders and bouncers may also simply ignore customer abuse.

In the end, it is often necessary for the dancer to defend herself. Dancers have several strategies to deal with verbally and physically abusive customers. (See figure 3, Taxonomy of things dancers do to get back at abusive customers.)

Before defending themselves, however, dancers often weigh economic considerations:

> When you get pissed off at them, you can go about it quietly; you can use a low tone of voice. You know, "All right, dude. That wasn't cool," or whatever. A lot of times that's not effective. The other way [screaming at customers or physically retaliating] isn't effective, but it gets . . . it's effec-

Things dancers do to get back at abusive customers	
	Throw bad tips in their faces
	Insult them quietly
	Scream at them
	Call a bouncer to deal with them
	Kick drinks over
	Pour drinks in their laps
	"Accidentally" kick them
	Hit them
	Refuse to dance/strip

Figure 3   Taxonomy of things dancers do to get back at abusive customers

tive because it makes you feel good, but it's not effective in that it doesn't solve the problem, really. It gets them the hell out. And a lot of times, that's what you don't want to do.

On the other hand, when another dancer reprimanded her for yelling at a mutual customer, Jasmine responded by telling her, "You do not need this disrespect for their two dollars. It's not fucking worth it. Where's your self-worth?" There are obvious limits dancers set for themselves to comply with a customer's demands, especially if those demands compromise her sense of self-respect.

Partly because of the need to cooperate as they cope with abusive customers, dancers often become close friends with each other and the bar staff. Although girls normally compete for the attention of customers, they will compromise their personal success in favor of having the support of other dancers. Jasmine calls the other girls and bar staff her family: "We take care of each other. We watch out for each other at work and outside of work too." In fact, although Jasmine claims that boredom and frustration have caused her to cut back on dancing, she is considering returning to the profession because she misses the people she worked with.

Conclusion

Throughout the interviewing process, one question I never asked (and therefore did not answer in this ethnography) was why my informants decided to become exotic dancers in the first place. The closest I managed to come, and the area in which my informants turned out to be most enlightening, was the question of how they make dancing worthwhile in a world that seems to afford them little respect.

The answer's details are specific to exotic dancing: with cultural knowledge and support gained from their colleagues, dancers learn the dress, gestures, looks, and moves necessary to meet their customers' expectations and the strategies to protect themselves against physical and personal abuse. Their motivation, on the other hand, turned out to be surprisingly reminiscent of how I've managed to make employment at my own mundane jobs worthwhile. Success for my informants comes with a simple focus on earning money, and above all, on preserving self-respect. Jasmine chooses to feel empowered as a dancer and, as such, advises new dancers to adopt an attitude of "complete confidence. Think that you are the sexiest, most wonderful female in the world." I like to think that is what I saw in Shadow the last time we went swimming—a newfound and complete confidence in herself.

Where Did the Time Go?
A Look into a Jesuit Pastor's Struggle with Time

Meghan Greeley

Our worlds are conditioned by the clock. Nowhere is this more apparent than in the work place, where the nine-to-five rhythm structures the day for many of us. Yet there remain occupations—midwives, farmers, clergymen— within society that defy this norm. Such is the case with Jesuit pastors, whose culture is the focus of this paper, for they are men who must balance their personal needs for rest and relaxation with a job that can easily demand their attention 24 hours a day. Priests are responsible for the physical and financial maintenance of a church, the preparations and performance of numerous religious services, including masses, weddings, baptisms, and funerals, and the constant possibility of a need to counsel and otherwise minister to parishioners with special needs. Given parishioners' expectations that a priest is always available, it is easy for members of a church to forget the person behind the priest's robe. This ethnography focuses on the fact that priests, despite their special roles in society, are people with their own needs who have developed a set of cultural strategies to achieve some *personal time* in a world that demands so much *working time*. Crucial to these strategies is the need to construct boundaries or limits in a world where few obvious boundaries exist.

Fieldwork

This project is based on a series of seven hour-long interviews with a Jesuit priest, whom I will refer to as Father Louis (the names of people and places are fictitious throughout the paper). In addition to these interviews, I also attended a church service presided over by my informant, who has been a Jesuit priest for twenty-two years and a pastor at his parish for six months. In approaching this project I had some general knowledge about Roman Catholicism, but I was unaware of the actual role played by Jesuit pastors. Due to the religious nature of the priesthood, my project could have led to an ideal view of pastor culture, but fortunately such conversation was limited, which afforded a better cultural understanding of what it is like to be a Jesuit on a day-to-day basis.

Jesuit Pastoral Work and the Struggle to Balance Personal and Working Time

Jesuits, priests of the *Society of Jesus*, are by training and vows ready to go anywhere and do anything. *Jesuits* may perform a variety of tasks in the church, ranging from teaching to evangelizing. Some Jesuits, like Father Louis, are appointed to the *Pastoral Ministry*, which means they *lead parishes* or individual churches.

The combination of expected pastoral responsibilities and Jesuit philosophy means that Jesuit pastors seem always to be "on-call." Thus, a central challenge in this microculture is the need to balance personal time with working time. In our first interview, Father Louis described what he calls his *day off* by saying: "There's always things to do. Even though yesterday was my day off, I didn't keep very good boundaries." Creating boundaries in this role is very difficult, as parishioners' needs for spiritual support and guidance don't fit within a typical workday's 9–5 time frame.

Pastors devote time and energy to a range of work-related activities. Each of these activities serves different groups of people within the parish, and individual pastors may prioritize these groups differently. Although this prioritization reflects more a pastor's personal view of his *mission* than a required set of expectations, pastor culture permits such choice, and choices are usually made within a framework of acceptable religious goals.

Due to the size and complexity of larger parishes, there are a number of groups (or ways to group) parishioners but the pastor does not have enough time to work effectively with them all. As a result, my informant has prioritized the groups within the parish in terms of how much attention he devotes to each. For a variety of reasons, he has chosen to focus on what he calls the "Generation X'ers" (young people) who live in the parish. He describes a goal of "trying to get a toehold for the Generation X in an otherwise very middle-aged established kind of parish." His reasons for doing so vary from the future being "much more fascinating to spend time considering than the past" to "faith-based, really wanting to make the Christian message accessible and intelligible to a generation that can easily become quite eclectic and relativistic in its spirituality."

Of course, by focusing on one particular group there are others that don't receive as much attention. It is mainly the older people in the parish who my informant pays less attention to. He makes it clear that he is simply putting a higher priority on Generation X than other groups in the parish, not neglecting his responsibilities to the parish community as a whole.

> I'm much more concerned about pastoring for the future than I am taking care of the past, and so I don't say this publicly, and I try to learn the names of all the old people. And I'm delighted to see them, but my creat[ivity] doesn't go, and so it's not as much a priority for me to visit an older member of the parish. I wish I had that energy.

Places to Pastor	Required or Not?	For Whom?	When?	Where Does It Take Place?
Confessions	R	All ages	3:30 Saturday	Church building
Daily *Liturgy*	R	All ages	5:30 Mon/Wed	Church building
Special *masses*	R	All ages	Varies	Church building
Saturday mass	R	All ages	4:30 Saturday	Church building
Sunday 9:30 mass	R	All ages	9:30 AM Sunday	Church building
Sunday 11:00 mass	R	All ages	11:00 AM Sunday	Church building
School mass	R	School children and staff	10:00 AM every 3rd Thursday	Church building
Classroom visits	N	School children and teachers	When has time	School classrooms
School board	R	School children	First Thursday of every month	?
Board of directors for school	R	School children	?	?
Special events at school	N	School children and staff	Varies	School building
Mass at nursing home	R	Nursing home patients	1x month on Thursday	Nursing home
Room visits at nursing home	N	Nursing home patients	Thursday	Nursing home rooms

(continued)

Figure 1   Paradigm of places to pastor

Places to Pastor	Required or Not?	For Whom?	When?	Where Does It Take Place?
Prayer services at nursing home	R	Nursing home patients	Thursdays	Nursing home
Hospital	N	Sick/dying	Varies	Hospital (usually rooms)
Parishioner's home	N	Whoever invites	Often Sat. evening	Parishioners' homes
Lunch meeting	N	Anyone	Lunchtime	Varies
Coffee meeting	N	Anyone	Varies	Varies
Pastoral council	R	General church	Third Thursday every month	Parish office
Marriage preparation	R	Engaged couples	?	?
RCIA	R	Adults converting to Catholicism	?	?
Confirmation prep.	R	Confirmation students	Sunday nights	?
First Eucharist prep.	R	First Eucharist students	Spring	?
Reconciliation prep.	R	First Reconciliation students	Spring	?
Committees	R	Varies	Varies	Varies
Ecumenical clergy meetings	R	Church	Varies	Varies
Archdiocesan meetings	R	Church	Varies	Varies
Staff meetings	R	Parish	Tuesdays	Parish center
Supervisory (1:1) meetings	R	Parish staff	Tuesdays	Parish center
Prepare couples	R	Engaged couples	Sunday afternoons	Parish center
Generation X'ers	N	Generation X	1x month	Homes of participants
Oxford forum	R	Adult members	?	?
Retreats	N	Participants	Varies	Varies

Figure 1   Paradigm of places to pastor *(continued)*

As evident from this chart, pastors shoulder a range of responsibilities. The difficulty in juggling these tasks is compounded by the unpredictability of some work-related responsibilities. For example, a pastor may have achieved some sort of balance between personal time and work time for a given week when a *parishioner* dies suddenly, requiring certain accommodations for various religious services. Clearly, as detailed in the chart above, certain responsibilities, such as mass, must continue as scheduled. This means that the flexibility in a priest's schedule comes out of his personal time.

Given these realities of the job, pastors must develop cultural strategies that help them to work efficiently to allow them to preserve personal time to manage their own physical and emotional health and continue their service-based vocation.

Time Management

One way pastors manage time is their use of the phone. There are many different ways that Father Louis manages phone calls. First, if possible he uses the phone to take care of the business rather than set up face to face meetings. As he says, "I just don't have time to have meetings with everybody who wants to have a meeting with me." He stresses that he is not trying to be arrogant in these situations, it's just a reality of time constraints. He also sometimes filters out calls he receives. If Father Louis receives a phone message requiring a reply, he may try to delegate the responsibility to a parish staff person. While difficult to do, he sometimes simply tells people he is unavailable:

> [A] staff person from [an interfaith social justice group] wants to . . . get together for an appointment. Finally, in trading voice mail messages . . . I said, "So what is the agenda? Do you have a purpose for wanting to schedule this meeting?" So, she calls back and says she just wants to get to know me; she's just stopping by and all this other kind of stuff. I'm tempted to call her back and say, "Mary, thank you, I'm honored, but I just don't have time to get to know people, especially this week."

Setting parameters around time commitments is also a useful way to manage time. Father Louis almost always schedules meetings with a starting and ending time because when the time is limited, business seems to be completed more efficiently, giving him more time to work on other tasks. He feels that if you have business to do, you should do it during the scheduled time, not allow yourself to waste time.

Delegating responsibility is a helpful way to manage time, but it requires follow-through. Key to doing this effectively is to prevent people from *pulling rank*, an idea that is supported by the overall structure of the Catholic Church.

> There is in the church what is a long-standing across the board principle referred to as the principle of subsidiarity that really tries and have decisions made at the lowest possible level. And it's not always associated

with the Catholic hierarchical structure that assumes that the Pope sneezes and we all catch cold, but there is a long-standing principle in the church that decisions should be made at the lowest possible level in the organization.

While delegating is an effective and necessary time management strategy for pastors of large churches, central ceremonial and religious functions can only be done by the pastor. For instance, custom dictates that the pastor must preside for Ecumenical *Lenten* services at an area church as well as the Easter Vigil Service at the local parish.

A problem many pastors face in dealing with time is their felt need to be everything to everyone. The inevitable solution is to realize that they can't meet this goal. It requires effort not only to know this but also to be comfortable with it. In a parish as large as Father Louis's, it is impossible for one individual to accomplish everything that could be done. Even with the implementation of time management strategies, there are just some things that will be left undone.

> I know of some people in the parish who really deserve a pastoral visit. One is a regular 4:30 mass attendee who is in the hospital right now, and I really, under ideal circumstances I'd love to be able to run down and see her. I just don't have the time to do that.

Pastors may also have to disengage when they simply cannot carry out every activity they have taken on. For example, Father Louis has been part of the Monday night *Ignatian Spirituality Group* this year but feels he must disengage and drop his participation for next year. This idea of disengaging relates

	Filter phone calls	
Strategies for juggling personal vs. working time	Delegate responsibilities	
	Be comfortable knowing that he can't be everything to everyone	
	Do self-care	Block off vacation time Regular physical exercise Journaling Fidelity to prayer Reading Allow people to take care of him
	Prioritize groups within the *parish*	Focus on Gen X'ers Turn down offers from friendly people
	Not allow people to pull rank	
	Set parameters around time commitments	Set starting time Set ending time
	Learn to disengage	

Figure 2   Taxonomy of strategies for juggling personal vs. working time

to the overall idea of being a Jesuit. As previously noted, Jesuits are known for their mobility and ability to go anywhere. "So, to learn that I can make a contribution—and that's a typically Jesuit thing to do—is to start things, but then to move on, to be mobile, to be able to . . . do things in such a way that it can be turned over to other people."

The Need for Personal Time

Father Louis, like all pastors, needs to find time to take care of himself as well as his parish. First, to keep healthy and vigorous he engages in regular physical exercise. It's important for him to find at least three times each week to exercise, usually by running, biking, or cross-country skiing. He usually exercises on his day off, a weekend afternoon, and one other day if he can squeeze it in during the week. Physical exercise makes him feel and sleep better, and gives him time away from the constant stress of dealing with people that is part of his profession.

Like many pastors, Father Louis has deep spiritual needs that he seeks to satisfy. One way to do this is to keep a journal in which he writes down what is going on in his life, and how it relates to his spiritual perception of his world. In the Jesuit sense of spirituality almost anything counts. Indeed, there are no arbitrary distinctions between the sacred and the secular. "We are to find all things in God, and God in all things."

Personal spiritual needs are also met by praying. Fidelity to prayer is something very important in my informant's life:

> I don't want to sound overly pious . . . but fidelity to prayer. In taking care of myself . . . I have to stay in touch with my primary motivation for doing any of this, and that's a faith commitment. And [the] primary, fundamental relationship or orientation in my life, which is a spiritual orientation and a relationship with God.

This emphasis on prayer has become increasingly important to Father Louis since he became a pastor.

> I've never had a ministry where my own personal spiritual life has been so exposed to the public. So, prayer and spirituality and spiritual rituals . . . annual retreats and other things like that, have always been important to me, but having become a pastor, I sometimes think, you know—Does every prayer, does every moment of retreat have to be open for public consumption or exposure? And I long for the days again when I can cultivate the [more personal part of spirituality].

Blocking out time for a vacation is also an important way for pastors to meet their need for personal time. Vacations for pastors may amount to a few days rest somewhere nearby or longer periods of activity enjoyed at greater distances. It's important to note that it's extremely difficult for a pastor to take weekends off since any vacation time that a pastor takes requires that another priest fill in for him while he is away. Despite this, Father Louis usually manages to block out the last week in January to spend time with old friends.

> And then this year, Jim, who's my friend, is the director of the Jesuit retreat house in Rhode Island, and he's invited me to come out and preach a retreat on Friday, Saturday, Sunday, and stick around Monday through Friday of the next week and come back here on Saturday of the following week. And the good thing about that is, it pays for my transportation. . . . So I have that blocked out. And I find that that works best—things really need to be blocked out well in advance.

It is easier for pastors to take time off on weekdays. This year Father Louis has reserved three days during the week following Easter to get away to a nearby abbey. For him, this provides an opportunity to relax, read, watch television, and disengage from parish events and activities.

Depending on Others

At times, pastors may find it impossible or at least difficult to take care of themselves, let alone their parishioners, or simply to feel the close support provided by a domestic group. When this happens, Jesuit pastors must allow others to care for them or at least help out. All Jesuits live *in a community* made up of brother Jesuits. In my informant's case, five Jesuits live together and one lives in another apartment but is still part of their group. This community is an essential part of the Jesuit life. As my informant said, he "can't conceive not living in a community, [he's] been doing it for so long now." The community provides support for its members, acting as a family where otherwise none exists.

> We're really there for each other. Like last night, after the Reconciliation service, I was down in the T.V. room, and I was eating a bowl of popcorn and drinking a beer, and Fred came down. And basically we were watching the sports report on the Fox T.V. network. But, what the stories were, there are some things that I remember about it. But it was an opportunity to sort of talk to one another, commiserate.

Beyond this local domestic group, there is also a larger community of Jesuits, of priests, and of other religious figures. The people in these groups have an intimate understanding of church-related tasks and empathize with one another. For example, my informant related a story about a conversation with a fellow priest:

> He was sitting there, and he was wearing ordinary clothes; no one in the church would even know he's a priest. And I went up to him and said, "You know, I'm not very well prepared for this homily. I know you're a superb homilist, how about if I just call on you?" He says, "Oh no, no, no, no, no." And he says, "It is just so nice to have this weekend off and be able to sit here." And we could commiserate and know exactly what

we were saying because I kind of get tired of going to church, or I get tired of presiding. It's just, I mean, I don't mind, I love the Church. I love the Eucharist. But I just want to sit and be part of the community; I don't always want to be leading the community's prayer. It's just been so long since I've been able to go to church.

This mutual understanding can offer fellow priests great comfort, a mutual understanding that their lay parishioners can't provide.

Conclusion

Most priests, ministers, rabbis, and other spiritual heads of congregations occupy roles marked by endless variety, the need to manage finances, organize and lead events, support people in need, and be on call 24 hours a day, seven days a week, and Jesuit pastors are no exception. Their role as spiritual leader of a group of parishioners is complicated by the fact that there are no clear limitations to what they can and cannot do, and when they must be available to other people. To deal with these expectations and lack of structure, they have created a system of cultural knowledge designed to ensure their own health and well-being, and by extension, the quality of their service to their parishes. Chief among these strategies are ways to limit possible tasks, efficiently manage those they decide to take on, reserve time for personal rest and "refitting," and fall back on communities of like-minded clerics. A Jesuit pastor is not exempt from the desires of average people such as time to oneself, or from the difficulties faced by many people, such as time management. Behind their robes exists a normal person trying to effectively manage time to best serve the church and preserve their well-being. As long as Jesuit pastors are not governed by a regularly structured and limited work schedule, they will continue to deal with these issues by tailoring their own job description and performances to available time. Even so, most of them will still be left wondering, "Where did the time go?"

"Alice in Wonderland"
The Culture of a Neighborhood Flower Shop

Sana Haque

Although often viewed as a "background" element for events such as weddings, funerals, and dinners, store-bought flowers and gifts serve important functions in American society. In a culture dominated by the ideology of the marketplace, people use the purchase of flowers and gifts primarily to fulfill social duties and satisfy emotional needs, rather than for their intrinsic value. The mission of all florists is to encourage and assist customers to fulfill these needs; whereas at large impersonal stores they are often provided with generic McFlower arrangements, small neighborhood flower shops permit greater individual discretion over the process. In this ethnographic study, I examine the culture of a neighborhood flower shop, ways in which it fits into the broader patterns of American culture, and ways in which it allows customers to creatively rework the rules.

Methodology

For my project, I chose to focus on one of the small businesses located down the street from where I lived. The shops there had always interested me, because of their (at least to me) eccentric, "small town" feel. A shop with an attractive window display called the *Garden of Eden Florists* (all names of people and places have been changed in this paper) immediately caught my attention. I soon introduced myself to a woman named Alice who was a customer service manager there. She agreed to do a series of eight interviews over a period of three months with me, all of which were conducted on the premises every Wednesday morning while she did her rounds. Although, at times, her statements were reserved because of the proximity of customers or other employees, this method had the advantage of enabling me to engage in participant observation and immerse myself in the microculture firsthand. The interviews were half an hour to 45 minutes long, tape-recorded, and then transcribed to form a written record I could analyze. I predominantly used the descriptive, structural, and contrast questions typical to the ethnosemantic approach to field elicitation, as well as a card-sorting game, to elicit detailed responses. The "inside" view of the store, its customers, and employee strategies represent my informant's manager culture, but much of her description is shared by other employees.

The Flower Shop

The factors that drew my interest to Garden of Eden stem from its unique social place in the neighborhood where it had been "on the same corner, same family," and the same street for sixty-five years. As Alice says, "it's not a franchise; there's not another one like it." The types of things sold there consist of flowers and gifts. I focus primarily on flowers in this paper, because gifts play a secondary role in the shop. Flowers are classified in terms of major holidays or other reasons for buying them (for example, shop employees may attribute sales to "love in the air"). I include a paradigm that illustrates the types of occasions for which people buy flowers, how they are categorized, and what attributes each one has (see figure 1).

The store is divided into areas that are scenes for various actions, including the "sales floor" (accessible to customers), "up front" (for processing orders), the offices (for bookkeeping and ordering), "the dungeon" (the basement), the "design room" (where "the designers do their creativity"), and the greenhouse (which holds orders pending delivery). Kinds of employees include the designers, who "do the big orders"; the sales staff, who serve customers and keep the floor looking good; the office staff, who manage the bureaucratic aspects of running the business; and the drivers, who make deliveries throughout the metro area.

Kind of Occasion	Are Flowers Essential?	Is It Creative?	Theme	Colors	Purpose Served
Halloween	No	Yes	"Ghoulish"	Orange & black	Fun décor
Thanksgiving	Yes	No	Tradition	Fall	Décor
Christmas	Yes	No	Tradition	Red, green, white	Décor
New Year's Day	No	Yes	Celebration	Depends	Status
Valentine's Day	Yes	Depends	Romantic	Red & pink	Emotional & status
Mother's Day	Yes	Usually not	Family	Depends	Emotional
Fourth of July	No	Yes	Celebration	Red, white, blue	Fun & patriotic
Confirmation	No	No	Religious	White	Décor
Easter	No	No	Religious	Pastels	Décor
Hanukkah	Yes	No	Religious	Blue & white	Décor
St. Patrick's Day	No	Yes	Celebration	Green	Fun
Proms & dances	Yes	Depends	Romantic/social	Depends	Conformity & status
Graduations	No	Depends	Celebration	School colors	Emotional
Weddings	Yes	No	Tradition	Depends	Status
Funerals	Yes	No	Tradition	Somber	Emotional
Birthdays	No	Usually	Celebration	Depends	Fun
Anniversaries	Yes	Depends	Romantic	Red	Emotional
Get wells	Yes	Depends	Depends	Depends	Emotional
Parties & dinner at someone's house	Yes	Usually	Social/celebration	Depends	Social & fun
I love you just because	Yes	Depends	Romantic	Red & pink	Emotional
Love is in the air	No	Depends	Romantic	Red & pink	Emotional
Need for color in the winter	Yes	Yes	Cheery	Yellow & spring colors	Décor
Dissection in lab	Yes	Depends	Scientific	Depends	Scientific
Theater stage	Yes	Depends	Depends	Depends	Décor (prop)

Figure 1 Paradigm of kinds of occasions

American Culture and How Flower Shops Fit In

My study of flower shop culture led to the realization that Americans seek to improve their social status or at least successfully validate their social relationships' rank through their ability to buy expensive items with no practical purpose. "If they want to make a big impression on somebody, they'll spend more money." As Alice says, "The more elegant and different it is, the more expensive it's gonna be, and people are willing to pay for that." Ironically, although people pay to be seen as "different," in practice they end up being mostly alike, in this case through the act of giving flowers. In addition, flowers are used as a substitute for emotional expression, denoting the extent to which the recipient is valued by the sender. The convenience of picking up a standard flower arrangement typically wins out over the alternatives of growing flowers by hand or spending more quality time with them.

An example that illustrates these functions concerns where flowers are sent. Some people who buy splashy arrangements for their partners for Valentine's Day have the order sent directly to the partners' place of work rather than their home. "During the week when it's for work time, the significant other, the sweetheart, will send flowers to their sweetheart at work. One, to vow their love; two, to show off and show people that they're really good." If Valentine's Day falls on a weekend, the flowers often get sent to work on the Friday before the weekend begins. Alice sees this public demonstration as a way for people to highlight their monetary success and engage in social "one-upmanship."

Because flower and gift giving serves to symbolize status and to substitute for emotional display, it is not the simple, innocuous activity many assume it to be. It is, instead, fraught with numerous potential pitfalls, ranging from customer memory lapses to inappropriate selection, several of which are examined below.

Potential Pitfalls

According to my informant, failure to obey social convention (whether through forgetfulness or willful defiance) has serious implications for customers (see figure 2). One of these is the danger of being embarrassed or shamed. As my informant states, no one wants to be "the only one [at the prom] without a corsage or a boutonniere." In addition, romantic trouble results from not giving flowers on an important anniversary or on Valentine's Day. "They always come in and go [frantic voice] 'Ohhh . . . it's my anniversary and I forgot!' or something like that. And then we give 'em a hard time and have fun with it."

Men are most vulnerable to being the object of resentment if they do not fulfill their obligations in this regard:

> School dances, you've got corsages and stuff that they reeeally need. If you
> have a date and he doesn't come to your door with a corsage, unless you

Pitfalls	Common Cause	Mainly Affects	Results	How to Cope with or Avoid It
Forgetting (social)	Memory lapse	Women— parties, etc.	Embarrassment	Good planning
Forgetting (personal)	Memory lapse	Mostly men— anniversaries, Mother's Day, etc.	Trouble with loved ones	Make-up flowers
Imbalance in giving	Unaware of rules	Everyone— Mother's Day, etc.	Resentment from others	Make-up flowers
Inappropriate giving	Unaware of rules	Mostly men	Embarrassment	Learn the rules
Giving unappealing flowers	Lack of attention to choice	Everyone— get wells, etc.	Embarrassment	Get help at the shop

Figure 2 Paradigm of kinds of pitfalls for customers

you said you didn't want one, OOPS. And um, Valentine's Day. You go out on a date, you don't pick a flower up, OOPS. Those are things that you reeeally have to [do]. . . it's a tradition, you have to honor the tradition.

An additional pitfall for customers lies in choosing an inappropriate product for the situation, such as cheery flowers for patients with a terminal disease. "If someone is terminally ill and they're not gonna live, you wouldn't want to send something bright and garish. You want something soft and pretty and loving." As this demonstrates, even sending the wrong thing on the right occasion can be a hazard.

The flower shop encounters hazards as well (see figure 3 on p. 144). The most serious is an occasional inability to keep up with demand during busy times, either because of late or damaged shipments or lack of available "bodies" (employees). "Hectic would be having to do all those orders and hoping we have enough flowers. Hectic would be hoping we don't get any last minute walk-ins that need 20 corsages." Offending customers or not satisfying their needs adequately, which stems from miscommunication or a general lack of attention on the part of employees, is a major concern.

Customer Service

Given the dangers inherent in the purchase of flowers, it follows that the flower shop employee's primary function is to use her cultural knowledge to steer customers toward the "safe shores" of appropriate gift giving and away

Problems	Common Cause	Mostly Affects	Results	How to Cope with or Avoid It
Lack of bodies	Unwillingness to work	Whole shop	Slow processing of orders	Pleasant environment for employees
Lack of materials	Bad planning & shipment problems	Whole shop	Unable to do orders	Good planning
Not satisfying customers	Insufficient attention/care	Sales staff, designers	Loss of business, bad image	Pay attention to customer needs
Inaccurate orders	Mix-ups, miscommunication	Sales staff	Loss of business, getting yelled at	Direct lines of communication
Messy appearance (shop)	Laziness, lack of attention	Whole shop	Loss of image	Constant picking up, motivation of employees
Failure to balance financial interests	Inattention	Owners, sales staff	Loss of image and customer loyalty	Follow maxim: Better give more than less

Figure 3   Paradigm of kinds of problems for the flower shop

from the "dangerous waters" of inappropriate choice. To accomplish this, she uses her extensive knowledge of social convention and expectations when serving customers. "I would ask them what the occasion was. If it's just a 'just because,' get well, or a birthday, I think of bright, fun, cheery, things like that. If it's an anniversary, then I think more serious, romantic, like red roses. If you know what the occasion is, then you can gear it towards [that, the occasion]."

"Grumpy" customers—those who feel obliged to buy flowers—pose a challenge to the capabilities of the sales staff. Some techniques they rely on to "convert" grumpy people include greeting them with a "smile and a nod" and listening carefully to their needs. "We have some customers who come in grumpy cuz they feel obligated to buy flowers for somebody and they're not necessarily willing to do that, and so you just kind of good-humor them and help them." Alice persuades such people to see buying flowers in a positive light by emphasizing the desirable end result of following conventional expectations, i.e., the smooth functioning of their personal lives. She admits that although "some guys aren't romantic" and "they just feel like it's a man's duty, they have to buy that wife a dozen roses," it is still a social good to instill in them the habit of buying flowers for their significant other because society has that expectation of them. "You know, to them it's a waste of money. The flowers are going to die. But it's better that they do that for the anniversary because if they don't, if they don't, then they will be in the doghouse."

Managing the Flower Shop

A number of strategies are required to manage the flower shop efficiently (see figure 4). One is to maintain efficient supply lines for resources and materials. The most important strategy for managers, however, is to ensure that employees remain happy so that everyone has an investment in the smooth operation of the business. The use of "Minnesota Nice" (a kind of cheerful, polite indirection typical of interaction in the upper Midwest) successfully masks hints of tension among employees, and constant cheeriness is the standard for behavior, with Alice using terms of endearment such as "sweetie" and "hon" when conversing with subordinates. For example, her

Ways for managers to avoid pitfalls	Guide customers appropriately	Match to specific resources	Appropriate style (creative or traditional) Quality equivalent to budget
		Explain social conventions	
	Keep employees happy and ensure loyalty	"Minnesota Nice" politeness	
		Inculcate pride in the shop	
		Pay attention to needs	Give extra hours for students Give time off when needed Make convenient routes for drivers Give creative freedom to designers
	Minimize lines of communication		
	Put customers in good mood	Smile and be cheery	
		Make special greetings for regulars	
		Pay attention	Nod and show interest Listen carefully
	Ensure adequate supply	Hire part-time help for busy seasons	
		Do inventory and keep records	
		Process orders ahead of time	
		Cover bases in case of failure	Have substitutes ready Warn customers of potential unavailability

Figure 4   Taxonomy of ways for managers to avoid pitfalls

response when an employee put a green plant in the wrong place was, "Sweetie, this doesn't go in the cooler. This is a green plant, so it goes up there. Only fresh flowers go in the cooler. I failed to tell you that." By addressing Molly affectionately and assuming part of the blame herself, Alice takes the sting out of her criticism. The good relations with and among employees benefit the store because nobody spoils Garden of Eden's cheery image by acting surly or unmotivated.

Customer Creativity

By emphasizing its neighborhood connection, Garden of Eden positions itself as an attractive alternative to standardized chain flower shops that lack attention to individual customer needs. The shop's customers, therefore, occasionally engage in creative reworking of the system, while staying within it. "Some people just want something unique and different; they don't want something traditional." The following story recounts a "game," featuring the use of a flip-flop sandal with flowers, which a married couple engaged in. It is a good example of how something unexpected can be substituted for the conventional flower shop transactions. "She'd bring it [the sandal] in and we'd make an arrangement and put this flip-flop in the arrangement and she'd send it to him. Well, when she'd least expect it, he'd bring it in and then we'd make an arrangement and send it to her. The same flip-flop would go flip-flopping back and forth."

Another instance where the usual sales rules were broken occurred when a man came in to buy his wife flowers for their anniversary. "It was his 36th anniversary and I was thinking, lots of roses. But you know, no, he wasn't into that." The man created a more genuine expression by substituting flowers he and his wife enjoyed. "He bought a really pretty mum, real pretty fall colored mum, and he dressed it up with a basket with fall leaves and cattails and a pretty ribbon and it looked really nice. So you can't assume it's always gonna be roses."

Conclusion

Independently owned, neighborhood flower shops like the Garden of Eden are a rare find in a world where shops have been sold to chains or forced out of business by mass marketing. In many ways independent shops serve the public in the same ways chains do, by providing flowers, arrangements, and plants for special occasions or as personal messages. But they offer more. They usually serve a neighborhood. They are friendly and personal. They permit variety in a standardized world. Still, to do this they must be large enough to meet customers' needs for products and to afford a management sufficient to order their products and handle employees. Garden of Eden is such a place.

As we have seen, it stands as an accommodating and personalized flower shop designed to help customers avoid the risks associated with the complex, rule-bound practice of flower and gift giving, while never losing sight of the importance of respecting cultural conventions and the social coherence and order they help maintain.

Dealing with Dickheads
An Ethnography of a Nightclub Staff Member

John Hoch

If you jam several thousand, mostly young, people into a small space and add alcohol and loud music, chances are some of them will misbehave. Such is the case with the crowd that patronizes Rock City (all names of people, groups, and places have been changed in this paper), a music club located in the downtown area of Center City located in the Midwest. Patrons and even band members (Rock City employees call troublesome customers *dickheads*) often drink too much, become abusive, fight, use drugs, dance violently, stage dive (jump on the stage with the band), or present false identification when they are underage. Handling them and managing disruptive scenes is the job of Rock City employees when they work *security* or *stage*. These jobs require some physical strength, patience, judgment, and humor. Employees need to control members of the crowd and occasionally the band without permanently alienating them. The club needs customer support and bands that draw a crowd to survive. This ethnography describes the organization of Rock City and some of the cultural strategies employees use to manage the behavior of dickheads.

The Setting

To find out about this culture, I conducted ethnographic interviews with my informant, Andy, a (more or less) full-time employee at Rock City. Twice a week for a semester I met him at the club for interviews that lasted from one to one-and-one-half hours. The transcriptions of the interviews and my observations at the club are the basis for this ethnography.

Rock City sits on the corner of Avenue A and G Street in downtown Center City. It appears as a black building covered with silver stars inscribed with the names of local, national, and international bands that have played there. The building is actually home to two attached clubs, Rock City and the G Street Bar, both of which host bands nightly. The club stands alongside bail bond businesses and empty parking lots among a large number of inexpensive semi-legal artists' lofts, which combine to form a center for the music and art scene. Rock City is a popular cultural centerpiece, not just a nightclub. The club provides a venue for many local and national bands playing a broad variety of music, such as punk, hardcore, alternative, hip-hop, world music, and ska. (Readers should note that music styles have changed somewhat since this study was conducted.) Ticket prices are low, which means large crowds, and there is no seating on the main floor so patrons can get as close to the bands as they like. Rock City also puts on *all age shows* more frequently than other music-oriented bars and clubs to allow underage patrons to see bands and turn into regular customers when they reach drinking age.

Most of the employees are also part of this music scene and are largely recruited from the customer base. They were *regulars* at the club when they were growing up, and when it was time to find jobs, they stayed in the music scene by working at Rock City.

> It's funny, when you are working the floor at a metal show, and you're in the pit and you're watching the pit and you are throwing out stage divers, that's the weirdest thing because I think, "Man, I used to be one of those." I've gotten thrown out of here so many times and now here I am doing the same thing.

Many of the employees are or have been members of bands, so they understand both sides of Rock City culture.

Rock City gives its employees the freedom to choose what and when to work different jobs at different times. Figure 1 (on p. 150), a paradigm of different jobs at Rock City, lists some of the jobs, and their attributes, which employees can do. Figure 1 illustrates the complex nature of running a nightclub. *ESM* (Entry Stage Manager) manages the G Street Entry, the smaller bar attached to the main club. This job is held by employees according to their seniority. *Tronning* is a server position and involves delivering drinks from the bar to customers on the floor. Among other jobs he can take, Andy is the only janitor, which is the sole day job on the list. *Door* means manning the entry

Kinds of Jobs	Hours	Pay	Dealing with Dickheads	Cold in Winter	Pretty Boy Job?	Starting Job?	Tips	Type	Carry Equip?
ESM	10	$5.50	Low	No	No	No	No	Stage	Yes
Tron	3–4	$4.25	High	No	Yes	First	$30–$40	Service	No
Janitor	4–5	$6.25	None	Yes	No	No	No	Day	No
Door	Up to 7	$5.25	Highest	Most	No	First	No	Service	No
Floor	2–7	$5.25	Yes	No	No	First	Yes	Service	No
Stage	12–15	$5.25	Low	When loading equipment	No	Yes	No	Stage	Yes
Barback	2–7	$5.25	Slight	No	No	No	$60–$80; $160 best	Service	Beer
Bartender	Up to 7	$5.25	2nd highest	No	Andy thinks so	No	$160–$250	n/a	No
Production	15	$9.00	Medium	No	No	No	No	n/a	Yes
LD	?	Not hourly	None	No	No	No	No	n/a	No
VJ	?	Not hourly	None	No	No	No	No	n/a	No
DJ	?	Not hourly	None	No	No	No	No	n/a	No
Kitchen	4	$5.25	High	No	No	After floor	Little; $110 club record	Service	No
Coatcheck	4	$5.25	High	No	Yes	First	Least; $9	Service	No
Telecheck	4	$5.25	High	No	Yes	First	Least; $9–$20	Service	No
Cashier	4	$5.25	Very high	No	Yes	First	No	Service	No

Figure 1 Paradigm of kinds of jobs at Rock City

door and *checking IDs* and, if necessary, *searching* people for liquor, drugs, and weapons. *Floor people* wash glasses, pick up glasses, and *watch for drunks*. The *stage people* help carry in the band's equipment, set up the band, and then provide security. A *barback* carries beer from the storage room to the bars.

Since employees, with few exceptions, work almost any job at the club and may even switch from one job to another on the same night, it is not surprising that the club hires generalists rather than specialists.

> When someone comes in looking for a job here wearing a suit and tie and says they want to be a soundman, they usually won't even get in the door. Why should they hire someone who just wants to work sound? We all have to do the shit jobs here, too.

Security Work

Rock City handles security differently from other music-oriented clubs in several ways. First, the club does not have bouncers per se; employees in several jobs handle security. I learned this firsthand when I entered Rock City to ask if I could interview a bouncer and was told that the club does not have any. For Rock City employees, bouncers are people whose sole job is to throw out unruly customers. Although employees working security at Rock City do occasionally throw out customers, they often use less dramatic approaches to deal with customer problems.

> One of the things is the way they work here, which is why I like it here, is you don't actually have bouncers, it's that we operate on numbers [of people] here. And just a lot of people coming and dealing with it. And we also operate on talking to someone instead of just immediately giving someone an attitude.

Dealing with Dickheads

Dickheads, as noted at the beginning of the paper, is a derogatory term used by employees to refer to certain customers and band members. Dealing with dickheads refers to everything from preventing members of a band from inciting patrons to stage dive, to checking patrons through the front door, serving them drinks, and stopping them from fighting. Most notably, it labels security problems that, with such large crowds of young people many of whom have been drinking, can be common and serious.

A number of jobs at Rock City require dealing with dickheads. Door is one example. My informant does not like to work door because it involves such a high level of dealing with dickheads. However, it also allows the staff to exercise autonomy and judgment, a freedom employees enjoy. At 7:30 each night, the employees working door station themselves at the doors before the club opens. At opening, they screen the customers who want entry by deciding if patrons are drunk, checking IDs for those who are underage, and, for some shows, searching people's bags and checking them with a metal detector. Drunk patrons are not allowed into the bar, so employees working the door must use their judgment to decide who is too drunk to enter. When Andy works door, he tries to see if patrons are slurring their words and if they are not giving him "straight answers" to his questions. If the doorperson decides that patrons are too drunk to enter but of legal age to drink, they may give out free passes to keep them coming back in the future.

Employees must also check customer IDs when customers look too young (under 21) to drink. This is another judgment call that may set off a conflict with customers, but fake IDs are common:

> I let a [black] guy in with a white guy's ID one night. I thought that was the funniest thing in the world, six [black] dudes and then I get one white ID and I was looking at no white people at all and I was like, "Ha ha ha ha ho!, who handed me this?" This guy goes, "Me!" I looked at it and [said], "Ha, ha, ha. OK. Here you go man [letting him into the bar]." That's fucking creative.

If employees see drunk patrons who are under 21, they may give them a choice of calling their parents or calling the police. Andy said, "Usually they choose their parents because the police are going to come and call their parents anyway." The doorperson must also judge whether or not a patron is *cool* enough to tolerate (and leave alone) other customers, because Rock City is supported by a wide variety of different and sometimes exotic patrons.

> You are letting people in that are going to have to deal with this transvestite in a huge fuckin' frilly dress, or this guy with a six foot Mohawk. If they are going to have a hard time dealing with it and they are going to have an attitude about dealing with it, then they shouldn't come in because that's the general atmosphere.

Employees working the door also decide what to do with patrons who have illegal items. The most common item found is marijuana.

> I grabbed a quarter ounce [of marijuana] out of a guy's pocket once and he grabbed onto my hand. I was like, "What have you got in your pocket?" And he's going (in a low growl), "Don't pull that out. Don't pull that out," and I had it. We were having this weird power struggle where I was like, "Oh ha ha ha, I got it out man. If I want this quarter ounce it's mine, you know that." But he was with somebody I knew. I said, "OK, just go, turn around and go away and come back without it, because I know you have it and you can't come in with it. I know that you know that I'm a pot smoker too and that yeah, you got it, but we're on the job."

Employees manning the door also have to use their judgment about customers carrying weapons. The most common weapon people carry is mace, but people have also been stopped for carrying razor blades, knives, and in an unusual case, a saw. Usually employees send the patrons back to their cars so that they can leave them there before entering the club. On several occasions when security staff were using metal detectors, customers noticed what they were doing and retreated to their cars to drop off their weapons before trying to enter.

Working stage is another club scene where security is important and dealing with dickheads is even more intense. In this case Rock City staff members must deal with a different group of dickheads, band members, as well as patrons. Many kinds of bands play at Rock City including punk rock, metal, rap, world beat, reggae, and pop. The type of band is not nearly as important as how well the band and its crew treat the Rock City staff. When working with bands, Andy says, "If they want to be dickheads then I'll be quiet the rest of the time. They probably won't get the best treatment. If they are really cooperative and really nice, they will get really good treatment."

The stage staff deals with the bands during both set up and loading. When a band arrives at Rock City, the stage people have to unload the band's equipment. After the equipment has been unloaded, the stage staff members set up the equipment on stage and get mikes set up for the show. All these jobs are easier if the band crew helps.

For stage workers, a good crew can make the difference between a lousy day at work and a good day. A few bands make things even easier for the stage crew. For example, Gagazi helped load and set up equipment themselves. Social Disruption dedicated a song to the security workers. Other bands, like Los Hombres, give t-shirts or sweatshirts to the staff. One band gave the stage workers marijuana.

A few bands are destructive and break rules, which makes things more difficult for the stage workers. Andy does not usually like to work with English bands because they tend to be pushy. A band with a large *draw* (meaning they bring many customers to the club) is allowed to be pushier with staff members. But this is balanced by one rule in the music business: you will meet the same people on the way down as on the way up, meaning that a band that is pushy with staff when they are rising stars will have to deal with the same staff when they are washed up.

The type of fans attracted to a particular band will change the work of the stage crew. Stage workers keep fans off the stage and pull down *stage divers*. The way band members treat the staff can also affect the way fans behave. Andy said, "[If] this guy [in the band] has been giving you a hard time all day, you are going to be a dick to his fans."

During the show, the stage workers position themselves on both sides of the stage and in the *barricade*. The barricade is made of either two risers or two folding tables that are taped together and placed on their sides with feet against the edge of the stage. When the band begins, three stage workers climb into the barricade.

> It's the most outrageous job. It really is a blast, because you have an unobstructed view of the band and of the crowd. Because you watch these people who are just getting crushed in front of you, and you are

like, "Tough shit! All I can say is this is your problem." Then you watch
the band from right underneath them and it's like they are talking to you.

Throwing out stage divers is the other main job of stage workers. A stage
diver is a patron who climbs on top of the crowd, gets on stage, then jumps
back onto the crowd and rides on top of the people below. Stage diving is
most common at punk, hardcore, or metal shows. Stage diving is viewed as
dangerous and therefore against club rules, but it is a typical behavior associated with this genre of music. Band members such as those in the Big Ska-
tones sometime encourage the crowd to stage dive during a show and yell at
the security staff for kicking out stage divers. If stage divers make it onto the
stage, they are thrown out of the club. This requires cooperation and some
physical strength and agility for stage workers. They must get through the
crowd to the stage divers, then pull them down off the crowd and get them out
of the club. Those who ride on the crowd without getting onstage usually get
a warning. Andy described his method for handling stage divers as follows:

> I got the secret down pat now. The way you get them down is you grab
> them by the back of their pants and pull them as hard as you can and as
> they come down backwards you get them in a headlock. And then, the
> extra added thing is, you start spinning them around and yelling at them
> so it keeps them completely off guard and they have no idea what the hell
> is going on so they don't have time to struggle.

Staff members joke about stage divers and attempts to catch them, especially
those who manage to elude the crew.

Stage people are also required to break up fights when they occur on the
floor in front of the stage. Some bands are disliked by the staff because their
fans are more likely to fight. Dealing with fights requires teamwork instead
of brute strength. If employees working stage see a fight breaking out anywhere in the club, they hit a button that triggers the *fight light* in the area
where the conflict is occurring. Fight lights are located on the club ceiling
and consist of six color-coded lights that look like they belong on a squad car.
When they light up, all available staff members are supposed to rush to the
area and break up the fight. If they try to intervene by themselves, which has
happened occasionally, they are likely to get caught up in the scuffle and
become injured.

It is possible for staff members to lose their tempers as they attempt to
manage unruly patrons, and it is easy but unwise to be drawn into a fight
themselves. If they do so they are fired on the spot by the club. Although it is
probably unwise, some employees take out their anger on unruly patrons by
taunting or "bugging" them.

> If you are that pissed off that you want to hurt somebody but you can't hit
> them, you piss the shit out of them, like [doing] anything—lick your fin-
> ger and stick it in their ear. It pisses someone off and it ain't gonna make
> the situation any better, but it's not gonna get you fired, and you get to
> feel better about it.

Conclusion

Anyone who runs a bar knows that drinking alcohol can cause trouble. When drinking is combined with extremely loud, throbbing music, violent dancing, and young people, the situation is especially volatile. Rock City features such an atmosphere and has created a loose, but effective, structure to manage rowdy and abusive customers, while at the same time avoiding conflict as much as possible with regular patrons. Employees are mostly young themselves and are drawn from the music scene they seek to control. They learn to look for trouble at the door by screening people who wish to enter the club. They often depend on regulars and friends who visit the club to vouch for and implicitly control strangers and they treat such people with more respect than strangers. They control band member behavior by refusing to help them if they misbehave, or by giving them special attention if they don't. They must be firm with customers and band members but sensitive to which ones are important to the club. Humor is a good way to handle the crowd and, among employees, a way to relieve the tensions associated with the job.

The employee term for unruly or at least "difficult" customers is dickheads. Since dealing with dickheads is generally unpleasant, staff members try to choose jobs in the club where interfacing with the crowd is limited. Working as a tron means little contact with such people. Working the door means greater exposure to dickheads, but working the stage is most intense. Despite such problems, employee culture provides them with an effective way to manage dickheads and keep the club under control.

Ethnography of a Legal Secretary

Jordan Pender

I want to suggest strongly that gender is not a mathematical concept. It is not a measurement of equality and should not be interpreted in an abstract, overly reified fashion.

What do I mean by this? I mean that you cannot weigh equality between people in the same way that you use a scale to weigh sugar or salt nor is it a monetary value, which can be put on the head of or in place of a person.

—Achola Pala Okeyo, Kenyan anthropologist[1]

Social status directs rules of social interaction, and it assigns people certain roles. In most cultures, especially those in complex societies, a hierarchical arrangement by social status is commonplace. In many cultures, status is related to gender, but as noted in the above quote by Achola Pala Okeyo, there is disagreement over how gender status is reckoned. In specific settings, is women's status subordinate to that of men? Or is it complementary, a separate but equal accounting? What weight do we give cultural insiders' points of view about whether their role is subordinate or complementary?

---

[1] In *Statement on Culture, Ethics and Ideology in Relation to Gender Equality,* presented at the Seminar on Culture, Ethics and Ideology in Naivasha, Kenya on February 8, 2002.

The position of secretary is an example of a gender-specific microculture within our complex society, since most secretaries continue to be women in this country. Such is the case for legal secretaries in most U.S. law firms. Like all social identities, that of legal secretary has specific behavioral require-ments assigned to it. Legal secretaries provide support for "their" lawyers and are thus in a subordinate position in the workplace. Since they are usually women, their role as secretaries says something about gender relations both in the law firm and U.S. society as a whole. This ethnography looks at the culture of legal secretaries in a midwestern law firm, with special emphasis on how their job is defined, their problems and adaptive needs, and how they see their job and their self-esteem. Of special interest is the different ways to deal with the male and female lawyers their work supports. Above all else, however, communication is a key to the legal secretary's job and a feeling that, rather than being a subordinate, she is a member of a team.

The Research

For several years I have been interested in how labor divides along gen-der lines. For this reason, when the opportunity arose to do ethnographic fieldwork in my introductory anthropology course, I looked for a microcul-ture that is traditionally thought of as "women's work." The culture of the secretary came to mind because it is such a stereotypically gender subordi-nate role in our society.

I began my research expecting to find that the world of a female legal sec-retary is a classic example of gender subordination, because her main role is to support the male attorney who employs her. During my research I discov-ered that I was partially right. The legal secretary I interviewed did see her main role as one supporting "her" attorney. However, much as Achola Pala Okeyo suggests in the opening quote, this ethnography of female legal secre-taries reveals that although their role is different from the male attorneys they work for, legal secretaries also work for female attorneys and, at least accord-ing to my informant, share a perception that their status is complementary rather than subordinate.

I used a series of social networks to locate my informant, Debbie Langer (a pseudonym). In order to observe Debbie in her work environment, I inter-viewed her at her office. She showed me around the firm and pointed out spe-cific areas of her cultural setting. Observing Debbie in her "natural habitat" had its advantages—Debbie was able to not only tell me about her job but also show me what she does. However, the fact that we were talking in a space surrounded by her coworkers and superiors may have limited the infor-mation she was comfortable telling me.

I soon learned that Debbie made a good informant for several reasons. First, she had worked at the firm for fifteen years, so she was well acquainted with the profession. Also, Debbie did not translate for me. Instead, she tended to speak to me using her folk terms, as if she was speaking to another legal secretary.

There were also some barriers to the ethnographic interviewing process, and I used several techniques to try to overcome them. Debbie seemed convinced that the culture of being a legal secretary would be boring to others and that I wouldn't really want to hear about what she does. As a result she tended to generalize and talk about the law firm as a whole, what the attorney does, and what the different departments do. I encouraged Debbie to speak about the specifics of her culture by always acting interested. By focusing my questions on certain aspects of her profession that I found particularly intriguing, I tried to convince her that I did not find the job of a legal secretary to be boring.

Debbie also assumed that since I was writing a paper for a college class, I would only want to know about the technical aspects of her job. She found it hard to believe that I would be interested in details like what she wears to work or the little strategies that conquer the problems of surviving the day as a legal secretary. I told her that I wanted to write "The Insider's Guide to Being a Legal Secretary" in order to invite her to touch on areas beyond the technical minutia of her job.

The Job

The legal secretary functions in a complex, hierarchical world made up of several cultural scenes. These microcultures each have slightly different goals, problems, and cultural strategies to solve problems and requirements, but they also work together to create a larger culture called *the law firm*.

The ultimate goal of legal secretaries' microculture is to efficiently complete any work the attorney needs done. However, the secretary has to deal with a variety of *types of people* and *departments* in the law firm in order to accomplish her own microculture's goal, including the *library, records department, central services, mailroom, accounting,* and *word processing.* As Debbie says, "We don't just deal with our attorney, we also deal with the other departments to make sure everything flows together." Secretaries work with different types of people as well, including *their attorney, other attorneys, paralegals,* and *nurse legal consultants.*

As noted in the introduction, secretaries can be male as well as female, as can attorneys. However, Debbie refers to the legal secretaries as "she." When she is speaking of the attorney in general terms she uses the pronoun "he," even though she categorizes attorneys as male and female when discussing what kinds of attorneys are easier to work with.

In addition to kinds of departments and people, secretaries do a variety of *jobs* and use several *resources.* For example, secretaries will sometimes have

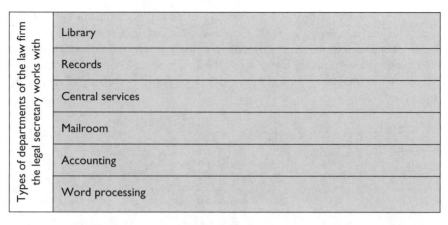

Figure 1   Taxonomy of the types of departments of the law firm the legal secretary works with

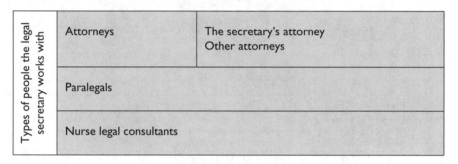

Figure 2   Taxonomy of the types of people the legal secretary works with

to do *library work, pulling a case,* or *accessing the database.* They also work with the *accounting department* to make *check requests, get money for a file, get payment for a file, enter the billing,* and deal with *American Express,* all part of her attorney's finances. She makes sure that the attorney has the money needed to cover a client's expenses and that all of the firm's expenses for a client are reimbursed after settlement.

The legal secretary also works with the *records department* to conduct *file checks* and prepare for *partner reviews.* The records department keeps track of the files the secretary is working on to make sure she does not miss deadlines. She also works with *central services* to produce *photocopies* and *fax documents* and with *word processing* to *get the typing done.* The secretary will bring particularly long documents to central services for *photocopying* or *faxing.* She will also bring long documents to word processing to be typed. The secretary *picks up the mail* and *sends mail out* from the *mailroom.*

There are also kinds of activities the secretary does on her own. These activities include *doing the mail, filing the mail, getting out letters, checking the docket* (deadlines for when documents are due), *getting copies, working on documents, doing labels,* and *requesting medical bills.* These tasks all contribute to the secretary's principal goal of getting work done for her attorney. (See figure 3 for a complete list.)

Kinds of activities done during the day	Doing the mail	Sorting it	
		Opening it	
		Dating it	
		Entering it into the system	
		Stamping it	
		Pulling a file	
		Putting a letter on it	
		Giving it to an attorney	
		Taking a mental note	
		Typing correspondence	Typing dictated correspondence Typing correspondence from an e-mail
	Filing the mail		
	Getting out letters		
	Checking the docket		
	Getting copies	Copying the article	
		Putting the article on file	
		Distributing the article	
	Working on ducments		
	Doing labels		
	Requesting medical bills		
	Typing	Typing pleadings	Typing discovery pleadings Typing substantive pleadings
		Typing depositions	Typing video-taped depositions Typing court-reporter recorded depositions

(continued)

Figure 3 Taxonomy of kinds of activities done during the day

Kinds of activities done during the day	Doing library work	Pulling a case	Looking up a book Photocopying the case Handing in a case
		Accessing the database	
	Working with the records department	Completing a form for a file check	Entering the docket date Putting it on file
		Partner review	
	Working with accounting	Check requests	
		Getting money for a file	
		Getting payment for a file	Bringing the check up to Lynn Applying it to the client's file Breaking down a settlement Distributing a settlement
		Entering the bill	Looking to see what file the bill goes to Stamping the bill Coding the bill
	Working with central services	Getting photocopying done	
		Getting faxing done	
	Working with word processing		
	Working with the mailroom	Getting mail	
		Sending mail	

Figure 3   Taxonomy of kinds of activities done during the day *(continued)*

Challenges and Solutions

As we have seen, legal secretaries must complete a variety of tasks each day in a way that best aids their attorney. However, secretaries encounter several problems as they try to meet this goal. One of the secretaries' main challenges is to make sure that they always know what their attorney expects them to do. Because of this, the secretaries partly judge attorneys on how efficiently they can communicate their needs. Debbie explained that on any given day, she is aware of what she needs to work on. "[The attorney and I] communicate back and forth to each other, so we know what needs to be done and when it is due. . . . It is never where I am sitting there going, 'Oh gee, what am I going to do today?' There is always just something to work on. You just know," said Debbie.

However, there are very specific ways that Debbie, or any secretary, "just knows" what she has to do each day. Each morning she checks her attorney's office. The attorney has an *"in" basket* on his desk where the secretary puts things that the attorney has to "review, sign, look at his mail, whatever." The attorney also has an *out* part of his desk, where he puts things for the secretary to pick up. There are different ways the secretary knows what the attorney wants her to do with something from the "out" part of the desk. The attorney will either have *notes* written on the work that explain what he wants done, or he will *dictate* his instructions on a cassette.

As an example of how attorneys communicate with secretaries, Debbie related an incident from her day: "Today, in the mail some pleadings—I think it was substantive pleadings—came in. He put a note for me to make copies for two other attorneys so they could see those documents."

Ways the legal secretary and the attorney communicate	Look at "in" work basket
	Look at "out" part of attorney's desk
	Notes
	Dictation

Figure 4   Taxonomy of ways the legal secretary and the attorney communicate

Legal secretaries categorize attorneys on the basis of how easy they are to work with. They view attorneys as good when they are good communicators as noted above, and when attorneys are not *difficult people*. Attorneys have bad communication skills, according to the secretaries, if they leave a heap of unidentifiable papers obscuring the "out" part of the desk. Attorneys are also bad if they fail to efficiently let the secretary know what needs to be done and they wait to give the secretary work until deadlines are near. The secretary cannot do her job if she cannot find the work that the attorney wants done or if she does not get the work in time to do it properly. If she does not know what is expected of her, then she cannot perform her job properly.

Debbie explains that "difficult people are difficult to work with; it is just common sense really." She describes difficult people as those who are *moody, blow up,* and who are *mean.* On the other hand, attorneys who are easier to

work with are *organized* and *stay on top of deadlines.* According to Debbie, secretaries at her law firm feel that "female attorneys are more difficult to work
with than male attorneys . . . you can ask anyone around here." She says this
is mainly because they tend to be more moody than the male attorneys.

Kinds of Attorneys	How Easy It Is to Work with Them	Moodiness	Keeps on Top of Deadlines	Organization	Niceness	Do They Blow Up When They Work with People?	Are They Difficult People?
Male attorneys	Easier	Less moody	Depends	Depends	Nicer	Not as often	Not as often
Female attorneys	Harder	More moody	Depends	Depends	Meaner	More often	More often

Figure 5   Paradigm of kinds of attorneys

Legal secretaries believe that the keys to being a good secretary are similar to the characteristics of a good attorney. They should be *organized* and
have *good communication and people skills.* They *ask questions* and *give suggestions.*
Debbie explained that a good secretary should ask questions if she does not
understand something, or if she needs something to be explained. "If you
think that what [the attorney] is doing isn't really how it should be, you
should be prepared to suggest a different way of doing something," said Debbie. She emphasized that *people skills* are essential. She stated, "Communication is the most important. I can't stress that enough. You need to be able to
communicate with the people *you work with.*"

Conclusion

I started my relationship with Debbie assuming that legal secretaries are,
by the very nature of their profession, in a subordinate relationship with their
bosses. Although this hierarchy is undoubtedly a part of law office social
structure, Debbie conveyed to me that this relationship can be one of complementary roles. If each performs his or her role, they can accomplish their
work effectively and efficiently.

At the conclusion of my research, I have no evidence that Debbie sees
her role in subordinate terms, let alone tries to subvert it. She sees herself as a
kind of mother figure to the often disorganized and sometimes unruly attorney: it is her job to organize his life. Just like a mother to her child, she can

better serve her attorney when he communicates his needs well. Part of her job is grooming the attorney to be a better communicator.

Similarly, the secretary judges her own success based on her ability to communicate with her attorney. Thus, question-asking skills are valued as well as suggestion making. A secretary needs to be able to ask questions if she does not understand what the attorney is telling her to do. If she sees that the attorney gives her flawed instructions she needs to be able to tell him so that he can give the right instructions, and then she can do her job properly.

The secretary has an assortment of behaviors that function to resolve the dilemma of figuring out what the attorney wants. The secretary judges both attorneys and herself based on how well they communicate with each other so that the secretary can better serve the attorney.

Coping with Stress
An Ethnography of Firefighters

Alex Rubenstein

Firefighters, because of their association with daring rescues, putting out fires, and saving lives, occupy a uniquely romanticized place in the social imagination. This idealized perception of a firefighter's world obscures the darker side of their job, stress and anxiety. Firefighters regularly encounter death, human suffering, and the dangers posed by fire. And the unpredictability of the challenges they face adds to their stress. There is never any way to know what will happen next, as a *call*, which could be anything from a paranoid person with a headache to a full-blown apartment-building fire, can come at any time and present a unique array of challenges.

This uncertainty combined with the anxiety accompanying their association with human suffering, the need to make instant decisions in emergencies, and the personal risks that accompany fighting fires and attending accidents, results in a unique kind of stress and a special part of firefighter culture designed to deal with it. Although firefighter stress is partially reduced by the professional knowledge they use to deal with their work, they cope by using a number of less formal anxiety-reducing, and often unconscious, strategies. Most of these occur in the *station*, a place where they find a laid-back atmosphere and camaraderie. In an unpredictable world, the station serves as a haven, a constant among uncontrollable variables. It also serves as the locus for discussion, counseling, and importantly, pranks, all ways firefighters cope with job stresses. The relationships that are forged at the station are central to performance in the field and the major focus of this ethnography.

Methodology

The events of September 11, 2001, put the spotlight on firefighters and police officers, and this undoubtedly influenced my selection of firefighters as the subject of this ethnographic project. Finding a willing informant was not a problem, but finding one who would be available during the semester was more difficult. After four trips to the station and encounters with three willing, but unavailable, informants, I finally met John (not his real name), who agreed to be interviewed. John, a firefighter in his mid-30s, was an excellent informant, often defining folk terms as he went through them and occasionally giving mini-tours within grand tour questions. Married, with kids, he has been a firefighter for about 15 years and at this station for the past nine years. I conducted seven interviews in all with John using the ethnosemantic ethnographic method. Each was recorded on tape and lasted about 45 minutes. Interviews were transcribed for analysis and they, plus my observations at the fire station, provide the data for this study.

Life at the Station

The life of a firefighter revolves around the station, which is located on a busy street that bisects a residential neighborhood in a midwestern city. Upon entering the station, you will find a main desk in front of you with another desk to the right. From here, you can see the door on the left leading to the *stalls* (the area where the rigs are kept). Just behind the desk is a staircase leading up to the *dining room* and the *cubicles* (where the men sleep). The second floor is also where the living room with recliners and a big screen TV can be found. At the back right of the stalls is a door that opens onto the *workshop area*. Through another door at the back of the workshop is the *workout area*, where there is a weight room and racquetball courts. When not responding to calls, firefighters perform a range of activities each week, as shown in figure 1.

The 24-hour shifts during which firefighters share all the activities of a domestic routine foster deep relationships and a strong sense of solidarity. This carries over into and is reinforced by what happens outside the station. The laid-back atmosphere of the station disappears in the blink of an eye when firefighters *respond to a call*. When a call comes in, firefighters morph into efficient machines, smoothly doing what they have been trained to do.

The station is occupied by two kinds of *companies*, the *engine medic-company* and the *rescue squad*, as outlined in figure 2. John is an *engine medic*.

Kinds of activities	Work outs	Weight-lifting Conditioning Racquetball Walleyball
	Training	Fire simulations Auto-extrication Planned training drills
	Cleaning detail	Cleaning the rigs Day-specific cleaning Monthly cleaning
	Food preparation and service	Grocery shopping Cooking Eating Card game to determine dishwasher Dishwashing
	Leisure activities	Relaxing in the cube Using a computer Watching television
	Workshop projects	Projects for the station Projects from home
	Pranks	Water pranks Baby powder pranks

Figure 1   Taxonomy of kinds of activities performed at the station

Kinds of Companies	Members per Company	Vehicles Used	Calls Responded to	Hours Worked
Engine medic company	4	Medic rig, rig	First response: Medic calls, fire calls Backup: Specialized rescue calls	Bi-daily 24-hour shifts with a 5-day and 4-day vacation each month
Rescue squad	5	Ladder truck, HAZMAT rig	First response: Fire calls, specialized rescue calls Backup: Medic calls	Bi-daily 24-hour shifts with a 5-day and 4-day vacation each month

Figure 2   Paradigm of kinds of companies

Unpredictability and Stress in Firefighting

Firefighters are thrown from one extreme situation to another at work. This dimension of the job is one of the reasons John likes his work so much. No two calls are ever the same, and there is no way to know what will happen next.

> I remember one time I had this call for a lady havin' pains. Anyway, we got there, and we got her in the back of the rig, and she is telling me, "Get it out of me, the aliens put it in me," and she was just talking out of her head, you know, so I wrote this up as psych just from the get-go, this is a psych call. . . . About halfway to the hospital, she just starts screaming in pain, and she says she's gotta push. She wasn't showin' or anything, but anyway, she keeps sayin' she's gotta push down there, she's got pressure, she's gotta push, so you know I'm thinking, she didn't say she's pregnant but you know, I'd better check. And yeah, there's a head comin' out right down there and she was havin' a baby . . . so I ended up delivering a baby right there, and uh, I would never have thought that that would have turned into that kind of call and I guess that goes to show . . . you just never know.

Although my informant has had many surprising encounters with happy endings, some have been much more sobering. For example, there are few things in firefighting as distressing as seeing a fellow firefighter get injured on the job. Everyone at the station is affected on both a professional and a personal level.

> I remember my partner and I had a house fire one time. We're crawlin' through there and of course you can't see nothing and next thing I know he's yellin'. We're up on the second floor and he went right through the floor because the fire had weakened the structure. He's actually dangling upside down, and he's stuck right there so we had to pull him out of there. He was probably out for six months after that, cause he pulled some stuff pretty good cause he was kinda like a pretzel stuck in there.

Although coping with the stress of the job is one explanation for the special atmosphere and close relationships developed at the station, there is also a functional explanation for firefighter solidarity. Each company is a team whose members need to work closely together when responding to calls. Trust and ability to work together are of the utmost importance. Furthermore, working together helps to create a support group to cope with more than occasional near-death experiences.

> I remember one call in particular where a car went off of this cliff and they rolled about 100 feet down this embankment. Their car was caught on this tree, just teetering there. We had a couple dead, and one who was in really bad shape. He was just about 20 feet under that car and we actually got up there to him, and we're working on tryin' to get him out of the way, and this car is just balancing on this little tree right above us. It was

just a split second thing, we went up there, and actually we went back to the station and critiqued this thing, and we're thinking that we were very lucky. We should have gone down from the other side and safe-tied that vehicle off before we went underneath and got him, cause if that thing would have went, we would have all been done for. That thing would have rolled right over top of us.

Stressful situations like this may come to be routine for firefighters after they have been on the job for a few years. Routine numbs the shock and stress of frightening and distressing events involving personal risk and the injury and death of others.

You get used to it. I mean, there have been a number of times where I was eatin' dinner, and right in the middle of dinner get a call and go over and somebody has died. You pronounce them dead and come back to the station and finish eating dinner. I mean you just get so used to it, you see so much of it that it doesn't even bother you any more.

Pranks

The vast majority of emotionally jarring experiences occur when firefighters respond to calls, and the timing and nature of calls are difficult to predict (see figure 3).

Firefighters deal with the stress related to calls in a number of ways. One is to talk with members of a *CISD team*, a group of firefighters, police officers, and doctors who serve as traumatic stress relief counselors. Another is to get

Kinds of calls	Medic calls	Attack victim Accident victim Cardiac arrest Respiratory problems Allergic reaction Abdominal pain Diabetic calls
	Fire calls	Structure fire Vehicle fire Wild (forest) fire Electrical fire Dumpster fire
	Rescue calls	Water rescue Ice rescue High angle rescue Auto-extrication

Figure 3   Taxonomy of kinds of calls

together with other firefighters after a call to discuss what happened. Just talking about stressful events seems to relieve stress.

But stress can linger below the surface despite these immediate structured attempts to reduce it, leading to tension relief mechanisms that are also more generalized. Primary among these is the way firefighters live and act day-to-day at the station, with its laid-back informal atmosphere, and an important feature of this atmosphere are the pranks firefighters play on one another. I believe that pranks are an essential part of keeping the laid-back atmosphere intact, and are an important coping mechanism for firefighters.

Pranks and joking may work especially well because most firefighters are men, and men (as opposed to women) often use pranks and joking as a way to structure interpersonal relations and manage hierarchy. (Anthropological linguist Deborah Tannen notes that joking and banter are typical in male conversation and communication styles that function to avoid the "one-down position."[1]) I believe they also serve to reduce the anxiety associated with the stresses noted above. Pranks are commonplace at the station. In fact, when I came to the station to meet John for our first interview, I was told that he was changing because his shirt was soaking wet. I assumed he had been working out, but soon found out that he had been the victim of a cascading pitcher of water that had been placed in a kitchen cabinet. As our interview unfolded, John recounted a number of different pranks pulled by firefighters on one another.

> A guy went over to one of the stations one afternoon while everybody was on a call. Their dinner table had a ceiling fan right over [it], and he put on baby powder, just caked the whole top of the fans in the kitchen and above the table. So about 5:30 dinnertime, he called down there and acted like he was one of the maintenance workers from the city. He said yeah, this is so and so from maintenance, we're gonna be replacing the ceiling fans so if you could just do me a favor and turn that on for me real quick to see if it's working. So of course he turned it on and he caked everybody at the dinner table there with baby powder. That was a pretty classic one there.

Firefighters should always take pranks like this in stride, because there is an unspoken understanding at the station that without them, the job would be much more somber than it already is. However, there are some unwritten taboos that may not be broken under any circumstances. Tampering with equipment is prohibited because a problem with a piece of equipment can endanger lives. Also, it is generally recognized that it is a bad idea to pull pranks on the District Chief. One of two District Chiefs in Sommerville (a pseudonym) resides at this particular station, and firefighters avoid fraternizing with him too much because of his rank. The captains, on the other hand, endure plenty of pranks despite their relative position of authority.

The use of pranks in the workplace might seem childish at first, but after one becomes familiar with what a firefighter sees everyday, the need for

---

[1] Tannen, Deborah. *Talking from 9 to 5*. New York: HarperCollins, 2003.

humor and a release becomes quite apparent. However, John also emphasized that what happens on calls and what happens at the station are completely separate. Therefore, one could return to the station after watching
someone die and have a pitcher of water spill on him upon entering.

> Once you get back to the station, it's back to station life. It's one thing
> that's kinda unique about working as a firefighter, especially working in a
> busy department, because you just learn to shift gears so quick. I mean,
> you can go on a dangerous or a traumatic call, but after a call is over
> with, it's done. You come back, and you're back to the normal stuff that
> you were doin' beforehand.

Conclusion

After 9/11, firefighters were featured as the unsung heroes of America.
Indeed, the terrorist attacks had a profound effect on the surrounding community's view of these men and women.

> We got a lot of respect and a lot of support from the public around here.
> Gosh, it seemed like everyday we had people in the neighborhood that
> would just bake pies and cakes and everything else for us and drop it by
> the station, you know, as a good gesture. We would do our normal shop-
> ping during the day, and people would come up and talk to you and say
> they felt a respect that they never really felt before.

However, the attacks on the World Trade Center had nowhere near the
same effect inside the station. "We all went about our normal stuff that we
always do. I wouldn't say that anything really changed there; everyone did
the same thing." So it goes in the life of a firefighter, where the unexpected is
expected and horror is just another day at the office, and the station is the
place to unwind.

The Modern
Pest Control Revolution

Byron Thayer

Pest exterminators perform a necessary, but socially unappealing, job. Responding, in part, to a growth in customer resistance to chemicals, the pest extermination industry has recently devised what they call *integrated pest management*, an approach that emphasizes a humane, environmentally sound, and pesticide-averse approach to controlling *pests*. This cultural model is rooted in a sophisticated understanding of pest biology and a distinctive arsenal of tools. This is an ethnography of the culture of pest exterminators based on my interviews with an experienced *pest control technician*.

The Research

Satisfying my curiosity about what was initially for me the shrouded and macabre world of pest control was difficult at first because I did not know any "exterminators," as I thought of them then. Resorting to cold-calling local pest control companies, I finally found Jacob (all names of people, places, and companies are fictitious), my informant. He is the technical director at a branch of Lanker's Pest Control located in an upper midwestern city and has had experience with all aspects of the business during his twenty-year career. I later discovered that part of his job is to coordinate some of the

172

public relations work for Lanker's. Jacob was intelligent, well spoken, and talked enthusiastically about his job, often responding to my questions with colorful descriptions.

I collected my data over a period of several months by conducting four in-depth interviews, taking an extended tour of the company building, and doing participant-observation with a second informant at two *sites* (a laundromat and a nursing home). All of my firsthand data, except information gained from participant observation, was recorded on microcassette and later transcribed. Parts of this ethnography are also constructed from my observational field notes. Portions of my analysis were based on the use of the ethnosemantic method, which focuses on informants' language to unlock the latent, cognitive organization of their cultural knowledge. Informant folkterms are italicized throughout this paper.

A limitation of this study is the number of informants interviewed. My main informant may not be representative of the pest control industry as a whole. Also, the fact that he performs public relations work for Lanker's may have influenced his description of the pest exterminator industry.

The Dual Faces of Pest Control—Then and Now

Most pest control technicians (PCTs) recognize that their job is unappreciated and misconstrued by the public as simply a profession that applies unsavory chemicals to kill equally unpleasant pests. PCTs feel this public persona is outdated and unwarranted, or at least inaccurate.

> Yeah, you'll find most pest control people are defensive about the word "spray" anyway, because when people call us they literally say this, "Hello, I've got some of this [fill-in-the-blank—can be mice, cockroaches, can be centipedes, millipedes, yellow jackets, honeybees, lions, tigers, doesn't matter]. Can you come out and spray?" The people kind of expect us to come out and spray for whatever is bothering them and I don't know exactly where that came from but the image is no longer accurate. Certainly there are many pests for which a sprayer is exactly the right tool, and then there's pests where a sprayer doesn't come into much use.

In the past, PCTs were expected to apply some kind of *treatment*, a broad term for pesticides, even if it was unnecessary. My informant told a story about how once when he was a *rookie* he did not apply a pesticide liberally enough and was later scolded by his supervisor because the client was upset that the place did not reek of chemicals. He grudgingly returned to the *account* and treated the place again. That was 1982. "The *sprayer-jockey* image is an old relic of the pest control industry." Indeed, even the term "exterminator" is being phased out at Lanker's as a part of the transformation of the business and their efforts to revise their public image.

Putting Knowledge into Practice to Manage Pests

In contrast to the sprayer-jockey stereotype, PCTs now operate under a new code of conduct that de-emphasizes pesticides. *Integrated pest management (IPM)* is the new way to control pests. The essence of IPM is to combine an understanding of pest biology with specialized tools to control pests in innovative ways without relying on pesticides. "You start with the pest and work from there. What do I know about this pest's biology and how can I bring that knowledge to bear on the insect itself? That's kind of the root of all integrated pest management." Today, technicians first try to discover the source of the problem instead of attacking the outbreak with a *broadcast spray*, the most generous dose of pesticide possible.

> Today this is probably better analogous to what a doctor does. Twenty years ago if you went to a physician and said "I'm really feeling anxious," and the doctor would say "Anxious? I've got a pill for that," and he'd write you out a prescription for Valium and send you out on your way. If you went to a doctor today and said the same thing, "Doctor, I feel kind of anxious," the doctor might pursue a more integrated approach, and the doctor might say, "I think I might have you see a psychologist because you have some deep-seated issues you have to resolve. You have to get at the root of your anxiety; we can't just give you a pill for that." [This is] the direction that the pest control industry has taken in the past 20 years.

The first two steps of IPM protocol, inspection and monitoring, are crucial in distinguishing IPM from the "old" model of pest control, because traditionally, spraying would be the first step. Today, spraying is looked upon as a last resort and should not be used indiscriminately. *Inspecting* involves searching for telltale signs of pests in places where they are likely to hide. Exactly where PCTs will investigate depends on the pest but can range from the more obvious corners to the obscure insides of walls.

Steps in integrated pest management	Inspect		
	Monitor		
	Identify "What is the problem?"		
	Make a decision	Don't treat area	Exclusion Sanitation
		Treat area	Select an appropriate formulation Apply the formulation

Figure I   Taxonomy of steps in IPM

> We walk into a room and think in terms of furniture, things against walls, and electrical appliances. Those are the three biggest cockroach hiding places. I might walk into a room and say that the picture on the wall is suspect. There's roaches behind that! And the little cracks and crevices that make up this table frame. Gotta look there for roaches, and that clock on the wall, the motor in that clock is about one degree warmer than the rest of the wall so there's roaches there.

Monitoring often follows an inspection, meaning small cardboard *zone monitors* are placed in areas where pests are likely to run across them and thus acting as sentinels for any pest activity. These zone monitors have a thin layer of glue that either leaves an impression where the pest moved or captures the pest altogether. In addition to zone monitors, a PCT uses triangle-shaped containers about two inches tall and nine inches on each side that they put in corners. Inside, the container is baited with slow acting poison, but more important to a PCT are the nibble marks on the container indicating pest movement in that area.

The processes of *exclusion* and *sanitation* are deeply entwined and are a prominent feature of a technician's expertise. Apart from actual pesticide treatment, exclusion and sanitation are the ultimate goals for a technician working within the IPM model. After a close inspection of where the pests are living and where they came from, my informant suggests ways to prevent (exclude) their migration. This may include steps as simple as keeping a door closed or changing existing light bulbs to ones that are less attractive to insects. Other examples of exclusion include *sealers* (cans of expanding foam) or *copper mesh* to fill a hole.

Sanitation is a specialized cleanup of an area to prevent pests from living there. "Clean up that floor under the dishwasher and you won't have the fruit flies. If you don't clean up that floor there's no amount of chemicals I can apply that will help you." Beyond cleaning, the term *sanitation* is connected to a PCT's biological knowledge of pests. Everything needs three things to live: water, food, and shelter. Sanitation involves the removal of one or more of these requisites. Jacob remarked, "My business card says sanitarian on it for that reason. I'm not just an exterminator but I'm also a sanitarian. Makes me feel better about myself."

Tools of the (New) Trade

The tools of a technician not only serve the function they were built for, but they also differentiate IPM from the old mindset of pest control. Pest technicians now emphasize *traps* and *applications* that are more humane, safe, and environmentally friendly.

In part because of the DDT scare in the 1970s, environmental concerns have manifested themselves in several ways, prompting the pest control industry to research and produce pesticides that affect the environment less adversely. Many of these are termed *biorational pesticides*, though the term is slightly misleading because some of them do not include a poison at all. Biorational pesticides are differentiated from traditional pesticides (figure 2) because of two general characteristics: their "living contents" and their low toxicity. I say "living contents" because many, but not all, of the biorational pesticides are actually organisms bred to destroy other pests. These usually come in the form of bacteria cultures.

Biorational pesticides always control pests indirectly. For example, bacterial drain cleaners do not necessarily kill the flies that have been plaguing a kitchen directly; instead they eliminate the filthy scum in the drains where flies breed so that the problem goes away. Jacob explained that if a manufacturer claimed that its product killed pests directly, they would have to register it with the Environmental Protection Agency as a pesticide, "which is no simple matter." Since biorational pesticides don't kill pests directly, they avoid this requirement. This loophole has been a key to the entrance of some biorational pesticides into the market. The other hallmark of biorational pesticides is that their toxicity is mild, making them an increasingly popular solution for pest control. Nevertheless, it is unlawful for a technician to claim that the treatments they use are "safe" or EPA-approved.

> Yeah [biorational] is actually a way of using insecticides in having no, can never say no, but having little or no environmental impacts. Everything is a trade-off though. You got a pest here that's causing damage to people's health and the environment, making the environment unlivable for people. On the other hand, we don't want to make the environment unlivable in other ways. . . . Or you can use a pesticide that's not a pesticide in the . . . normal conception of the word, which is "highly toxic chemical leaking in a drum in a landfill somewhere, with a skull and crossbones on it."

During my tour of the warehouse, Jacob showed me a specialized mousetrap that is now a standard tool. The highlighted feature of the mousetrap is its humane approach to killing the mouse without causing unnecessary suffering. This *humane trap* also makes use of what is known about mouse behavior: if mice see a tunnel, they will investigate it. Therefore, this trap uses a dark passageway that leads toward a killing contraption,

> . . . and this thing comes down across about the fourth cervical vertebrae. This is listed under the American Veterinary Medical Association's list of acceptable ways to, um, humanely [dispose] of mice: cervical dislocation. That's what happens when you go into the trap this way. Now, if the trigger were facing out this way it comes down on its claw and he'd have to chew his foot off and bleed and it would get infected and suffer for a while. [At a different point Jacob explained that traditional mousetraps sometimes have this problem.] The thing is, when they tunnel this way there is no half way, he's totally committed and he hits the trigger and dies instantly.

	Traditional tools	Pesticide formulations	Sprays	Wettable powder Soluble powders Emulsified concentrates Oil soluble concentrates
Tools to treat an area			Granulars	
			Baits	
			Dusts	
		Non-formulation applications	Resin strips	
			Sticky boards	
	Integrated pest management (IPM) tools	Biorational pesticides		
		Humane traps		
		Biorational traps		

Figure 2   Taxonomy of tools to treat an area

Biorational traps are perhaps the most ingenious and amusing tools in a PCT's repertoire. These traps capitalize on biological pest knowledge, including eating and mating habits, more than other techniques. Jacob showed me a device to control *Indian Mill Moths* that contained a strip of glue impregnated with moth sex pheromones. Moths are tricked into seeking companionship and become trapped in the glue. A variation of the glue strip is used as an alternative to mothballs when packing goods for long periods of time. Other curious baits to control pests include mint jelly and peanut butter.

Another example of a biorational trap is the *growth regulator,* which is applied to cockroaches to alter their growth patterns. For a period of time when a female roach is bearing an egg capsule, she will not eat and will not move from where she is, making an application of tasty bait useless. A *growth regulator* emulates a growth hormone and fools female roaches into eating (including the tasty bait) when they normally avoid food. Incidentally, growth regulators were originally developed and marketed as birth control for roaches. Other pesticides are applied to ants using the behavioral knowledge that they will retrieve food and carry it back to the nest, the communal stomach, where they regurgitate it for the nourishment of the worker ants and larvae. In this way, a slow-acting poison can permeate the entire nest.

Conclusion

Unknown to many, pest control technicians have developed integrated pest management, an innovative approach that better copes with the socially unappealing qualities inherent in controlling pests. Although rhetoric like this might be interpreted by some as simply a face change for the industry, this is not the case. PCTs recognize the public's ambivalence about their profession and have struggled to address their clients' apprehension. The result is a pest control approach that relies heavily on technicians' knowledge of pest biology as well as a clever and specialized selection of tools that are environmentally friendly and humane as well as effective.

Catching Babies
An Ethnography of a
Licensed, Traditional Midwife

Natasha Winegar

Every culture has different rituals and beliefs regarding childbirth that shape a woman's birth experience. Women in some cultures isolate themselves during childbirth while others migrate to a central location such as a birthing center to seek professional assistance during labor. In the United States, women usually give birth in the hospital or, less commonly, the home, and they seek the assistance of a birthing specialist, a doctor or a midwife. While both kinds of birthing specialists strive to provide the best possible care, how their roles are defined and implemented varies according to the cultural norms of each practitioner group. Although hospital-based birth attended by a doctor constitutes the societal norm in the U.S., this ethnography looks at the microculture of midwifery (more specifically licensed, traditional midwifery) as an established alternative birth option that more and more families are embracing.

Most licensed, traditional midwives believe that there are problems with the way birth is conceptualized in the medical institutional context. They maintain that the care provided by doctors attending birth in the hospital places too much emphasis on the physical aspects of pregnancy and labor. As a result midwives believe that the way birth is treated in this context is overly

179

medical. In contrast, midwives strive to provide alternative care to families, which differs in terms of the space in which this care is located, the holistic framework that structures it, and the types of relationships midwives build with those whom they are helping.

The alternative care provided by midwives is an attempt to resist or at least replace standard medical practices. However, licensed, traditional midwives believe that in order to provide adequate care for their families they must be able to interface and maintain contact with the medical establishment. These attempts to work with the medical establishment sometimes cause conflict for midwives. However, because their goal ultimately is to benefit the women with whom they work, they have developed cultural strategies for negotiating tensions with the medical establishment.

Methodology

My interest in midwifery is part of a much broader engagement with women's health. Prior to this project, I had completed research on a variety of topics pertaining to women's health, the majority of which focused on the health-care industry. I became interested in midwifery as an alternative to institution-based health care.

My informant, Molly (not her real name), is a middle-aged woman who is married and has three children. She is a licensed, *traditional* midwife, has been doing midwifery for almost twelve years, and has her own *home birth practice*. She primarily works out of her home, but her work setting also encompasses other midwives' homes, mothers' homes, and the hospital.

Despite her busy schedule, Molly and I met for an hour once a week for eight weeks. With Molly's consent, I recorded all of our interviews. After each interview I transcribed the full interview and recorded any field notes I had taken. I used the Spradley-McCurdy method of ethnographic interviewing and as such my first interviews were broader in terms of the type of information they covered. As the interviews progressed they elicited more detailed information.

I experienced few problems while conducting this research and those that I encountered gave me greater insight into the culture of midwifery. For example, Molly missed a few of our scheduled interviews. At first, this caused some concern, as I questioned Molly's interest in working with me. Once I learned that she missed our appointment because she was needed at a birth, I was able to understand firsthand something that Molly had repeatedly mentioned: midwives do not simply consider midwifery their job; it touches and is a part of every aspect of their lives.

Home Birth in the Home: "Midwives Still Do House Calls"

Since the essence of midwifery is home birth, it is not surprising that the home is the major work setting. My informant's home birth practice is located in her house, but the birth and most of the postpartum visits occur in the family's home. Midwives believe that the medical industry's overemphasis on the clinical aspects of care prevents doctors from feeling that they can provide adequate care in the home. Traditional midwives feel that women should receive care in a *safe* and *comfortable* space, and that the home is the best environment in which to achieve this goal.

At home, women are able to create a *birth plan*, in which they describe whom they want to *attend the birth* and each family member's role at the birth. The key here is that midwives believe that *labor* goes more smoothly if parents are allowed some privacy during the birth. This contrasts with hospital births, where families are afforded scant privacy and little say over who is present at the birth.

The home setting is a large part of what makes midwifery unique within the realm of health care and is foundational in how midwives define midwifery, birth, and the type of care that they provide. The following section details the type of care that midwives offer families.

Holistic Care

Since the alternative care of licensed, traditional midwives is an attempt to resist the sterility that is characteristic of hospital care, it is essential to understand some of the differences in activities and beliefs between midwives and doctors. Some of the major differences are identified in the kinds of activities involved in providing care during childbirth in figure 1 (on p. 182).

Figure 1 details what comprises "holistic" care, a central tenet of midwifery, as Molly describes in the following quote:

> So right away I got signs that she was going to be a very good apprentice because she was not separating life from midwifery; she was just doing whatever needed to be done, which is pretty much what midwifery is.

Midwives believe doctors focus their care solely on the physical needs of women, which separates care from a mother's emotional or spiritual needs. This results in hospital births being overly medical. Central to midwifery is the idea of a holistic care that extends beyond a woman's physical needs. Midwives believe that they do not separate their care from "life"; life refers to all the other things associated with birth and pregnancy, such as a woman's or family's changing emotions and support systems. This cultural belief affects and is extended to all types of care that midwives administer, including *prenatal* and *postpartum* care and care provided during birth. My interviews elicited

Kinds of Activities	Dimensions of Contrast	
	Traditional Midwife	Doctor
"Catches" a baby	Yes	No
"Delivers" a baby	No	Yes
Does home visits	Yes	No
Calls moms at home	Yes	No
Uses herbs	Yes	No
Provides holistic care	Yes	No
Takes the baby from the mom after birth	No	Yes
Calls out the sex of the baby	No	Yes
Fights for credentials	Yes	No
Expends a lot of energy on prenatals	Yes	No
Works at home	Yes	No
Comes to the birth just for the delivery	No (unless that is what the mom wants)	Yes
Does 15-minute prenatal visits	No	Yes
Gives the family some privacy after the birth	Yes	No
Uses machines and scalpels	No	Yes
Has an agenda about what needs to get done	No (although there are some tasks she needs to do)	Yes
Do 6–12 births a day	No	Yes
Has a partner	Yes	Maybe
Has a professional education ("real")	Maybe	Yes
Yells directives while a mom is pushing	No	Yes
Cuts the umbilical cord immediately	No	Yes
Promises a perfect outcome	No	Yes (however, this is being done now with less frequency)
Promotes a mother's responsibility for her health and information	Yes	No
Talks about pain prenatally	Yes	Maybe
Explains the medical tools being used	Yes	No
Relies on diagnostics	No	Yes
Has to carry malpractice insurance	No	Yes
Has to deal with burnout	Yes	Maybe

Figure I Partial paradigm of kinds of activities done by doctors and midwives

a wealth of examples demonstrating this concept of *holism*. Here I focus on prenatal care as an example.

Midwives feel that good prenatal care is essential to both the mother's and baby's health. In the hospital, prenatal visits average about fifteen minutes in length; a midwife's *prenatals* are generally one to two hours long. Molly felt that this extended time allowed her to attend to more than just the physical aspects of care and to form a relationship with the woman, which she felt is essential to a good prenatal. The activities done at a prenatal are outlined in figure 2 on pp. 184–186.

The *visit* portion of the prenatal takes up the majority of the prenatal and involves all other aspects of care important to midwives. This includes discussing the emotional, educational, and support needs of the *mom* and *family*. Most importantly, it includes envisioning the birth and the mom's expectations of it. Although there is no real structure to this portion of the prenatal, it frequently involves questions such as, "What are you feeling about the birth?"

One of the most important topics discussed during the visit portion of the prenatal is *catching* the baby: Who is catching it? When should he or she catch it? How they should catch it? The quote below illustrates the difference between home birth catching and hospital birth and helps illustrate midwives' concept of holistic care. It also highlights how midwives see their approach in opposition to that of the medical establishment.

> Midwives are fanatic about the word *deliver*. They don't deliver. They will catch a baby. You know, they will hold your butt. It is really important, if you say deliver to a woman, I feel like you are telling her that you are going to get her baby out, and you are not. Nobody can do that. So it crystallizes for you, you'll realize with a little anxiety perhaps, oh my god, I have to get this out and I am not sure if I can and it hurts and I don't know if I can do this. It is a classic turning point in labor. Usually we call it a "reckoning" and that is when the woman goes and goes for it and pushes it.

This stressing of the mother's role in the birth is important, but midwives do not try to overwhelm mothers with this knowledge. Instead, they provide them with support by building a close relationship with them, as discussed in the next section.

Nonhierarchical Relationships

Midwives maintain that the medical establishment creates a hierarchical relationship between doctors and mothers. Embedded in this relationship is the idea that doctors know more about the woman's body and pregnancy than she does. In contrast, midwifery is defined in more egalitarian terms as simply an extension of mothering, or a "mom-to-mom basis." Midwives believe that their job is to help empower women by providing them with

Activities done at prenatal visits			
Arrive	Apprentice sets everything up	Puts teapot on	
		Makes tray of snacks	
		Gets chart ready	
	Family comes		
Do clinical/physical stuff	Check blood pressure		
	Do a pelvic exam (done once at one of the last prenatals)		
	Have mom pee on urine sticks	Check sugar	
		Check protein	
	Listen to the baby's heart rate	Midwife listens	
		Family listens	
		Take pictures of the family listening	
	Measure the mom's belly and check on baby's growth rate		
	Ask screening questions	Ask about nausea	
		Ask about sleep	
		Ask about headaches	
		Ask about visual disturbances	
		Ask about poop	
		Ask about pee	
		Ask about swelling	Ask about swelling in the face
			Ask about swelling in the feet
			Ask about swelling in the hands

(continued)

Figure 2 Compound taxonomy of kinds of activities done at a prenatal visit

Activities done at prenatal visits			
Do clinical/physical stuff (continued)	Palpate the baby	Wash hands	
		Check the warmth of her hands	
		Let the mom feel her hands	
		Put her hand on the mom's belly for 30 secs.	
		Rub the baby	
		Say "hi baby"	
		Feel for the baby's position by searching for certain landmarks	Feel for head
			Feel for back
			Feel for butt
		Talk about what you're feeling	
		Ask the mom what she has been feeling	
		Make connection between what you're feeling and what the mom has been feeling lately	
Take care of kids	Feed them snacks		
	Change diapers		
Have the visit	Discuss how the parents are getting along		
	Provide childbirth education (childbirth education includes a huge variety of things; however, due to constraints they are not expanded upon here)		
	Take a history (done on first visit)	Ask about lifestyle	
		Ask about detailed medical history	

(continued)

Figure 2 Compound taxonomy of kinds of activities done at a prenatal visit (continued)

Activities done at prenatal visits	Have the visit (continued)	Discuss various checklist items on inside cover of chart/childbirth education checklist		
		Make a two-week diet plan		
		Discuss if the parents need anything from each other		
		Discuss what to do about other children at the birth	Discuss if mom wants her other children at the birth	
			Discuss if mom wants someone there to take care of them	
		Find out what the mom has been thinking about		
		Find out about the mom's dreams		
		Find out about her fears		
		Talk about the mom's feelings about the birth		
		Talk about fears		
		Find out about the support she's receiving for her plans for home birth	Find out about support from her family	
			Find out about other support	

Figure 2 Compound taxonomy of kinds of activities done at a prenatal visit *(continued)*

friendship, advice, mentoring, and the encouragement to be responsible for their own health and pregnancy.

Midwives believe that a potential negative outcome of the medicalized relationship between doctors and pregnant women is that women become complacent, assuming their doctor will take responsibility for their health. This can discourage families from taking responsibility for their own health and understanding what they can do to ensure a healthy pregnancy.

Support and Interfacing with the Medical Establishment

Much of this paper has illustrated how midwives see themselves as different from, and even in opposition to, standard medical practices. However, to provide adequate care for all mothers licensed, traditional midwives must be comfortable working with doctors in the hospital setting. My informant states, "It's extremely important to me, personally, that I can work and interface with medicine really well so that there are no gaps in my families' care." Many challenges arise from the seeming contradiction of resisting, yet working within, institutional medicine. Midwives have developed cultural strategies to address these challenges by finding support from partners, apprentices, and the home birth community.

Establishing a *back-up doctor* is one of the most important ways that midwives seek to ensure continuity of care for their mothers. However, it is also one of the most challenging. Doctors are critical of midwifery and frequently apprehensive about the implications of working with a midwife. Paradoxically, calling a doctor for help forces midwives to confront many of the same obstacles and problems they seek to avoid by being a midwife. Upon entering hospitals, midwives immediately meet head-on a hierarchy that devalues their knowledge and area of expertise. Nurses and doctors usurp the midwife's authority as soon as care for the mother is transferred to the medical realm. Midwives have developed many strategies for dealing with these complicated relationships.

For example, many licensed, traditional midwives, like Molly, are formally trained as nurses and are well versed in medical language. They deploy this knowledge when speaking with doctors, even though they don't use this language with the women under their care. In this setting, therefore, midwives refer to a woman as a "patient" instead of a "mom." Although midwives feel that they must compromise some of their beliefs when entering a hospital, this ability to walk in both worlds allows them to ensure that moms receive the care they need.

Outside the hospital midwives have other strategies to deal with this devaluation of their skills and knowledge by the established medical community. A key strategy is to maintain relationships with others in the *home birth community,* which in its broadest sense is an informal network of midwives, home birth families, and *home birth supporters.* A more formal network can be seen in the state midwife community. It encompasses many different styles (depicted below in figure 3) of midwifery and represents the degree to which each interfaces with the medical establishment.

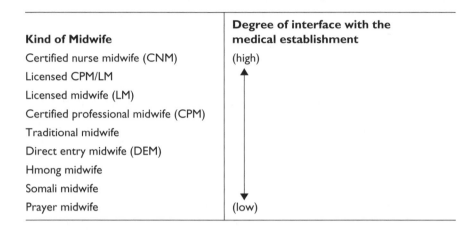

Kind of Midwife	Degree of interface with the medical establishment
Certified nurse midwife (CNM)	(high)
Licensed CPM/LM	
Licensed midwife (LM)	
Certified professional midwife (CPM)	
Traditional midwife	
Direct entry midwife (DEM)	
Hmong midwife	
Somali midwife	
Prayer midwife	(low)

Figure 3   Continuum of the degree to which different kinds of midwives interface with the medical establishment

My informant described this scale in terms of the degree to which midwives choose to interface rather than how medical or technical they are because, as she stated, "When you call a midwife medical, you know, you are going to raise some hackles 'cause they are concerned with how medicalized birth has become so they don't want to be called medical; those are basically fighting words." However, as figure 3 indicates, a greater degree of technical/ medical knowledge correlates with a higher degree of interfacing.

Not all midwives choose to interface with the medical establishment because they distrust and are skeptical about it. Licensed, traditional midwives appear in the middle of the spectrum, as they are licensed and some have been to nursing school. Licensure provides them with some credibility and respect when they deal with the medical establishment.

The home birth community is politically divided over the amount of support it provides each type of midwife. The issue involves a conflict over licensure, whether it should be required, and who, midwives or others, should do the licensing. The attributional differences among midwives most involved in this debate are illustrated in figure 4.

Despite the debate about licensure and the differences in the type of care that each midwife provides, the home birth community provides a system of support for all midwives. As my informant maintained, all midwives hold a few important and cultural attributes: they are practical and they have faith in their *moms*. My informant feels that *faith* is the main element of midwifery

Kinds of Midwives	Technical	Bring Own Families to Docs	Live Quietly in Own Niche	Approve of Regulation and Licensure	Home School Their Kids	Volume of Practice	Take Risks	Will Transfer Care to Hospital	Will Transfer Care to Home	Labeled as "Dangerous"	Licensed Regionally/Nationally	Conservative	Politically Active	Do Labor Support in Hospital
No CPM or license	Very low-tech	No	Yes	No	Yes	High	Yes	No	Yes	Yes	No	No	No	No
CPM	Low-tech	Maybe	Maybe	A little	Maybe	Medium	Maybe	Maybe	Maybe	Maybe	Nationally	In between	Maybe	Maybe
CPM/LM	Technical	Yes	No	Yes	Maybe	Medium	No	Yes	No	No	Both	Yes	Yes (although they don't like it)	Yes

Figure 4 Attributes of midwives involved in licensing debate

and thus it is what holds the community together. She stated that "practical is what midwifery is and medicine is not."

Conclusion

Traditional, licensed midwives attempt to provide alternative care to moms and families who do not wish to give birth in the hospital. In many ways, home birth is a resistance to the medicalization of birth, which the medical establishment perpetuates. The type of care midwives provide is an alternative. First, it is holistic in that it does not rely on diagnostics and clinical assessments as extensively as doctors' care does. Although midwives provide clinical care, they lend equal importance to the things that affect physical health, such as emotions, environment, and support.

Second, midwives stress the importance of the home as an integral part of holistic care. In this way, they believe, care is more intimate and personal because the mother and her family members participate in shaping care to meet their own needs. Midwives feel that families are receiving the best possible care when they are in the home because it is sculpted to suit their needs. For them, a hospital agenda cannot do this.

Lastly, midwives resist the medical establishment by opposing the hierarchy present in the medical world. Midwives feel that doctors assume a relationship of authority with their patient, inherently causing moms to become passive. In an attempt to counter this, midwives encourage a more egalitarian relationship with mothers and their family members. They encourage moms to be responsible for their own health and information and attempt to empower them in the birth process, a sense of control midwives believe is absent in the hospital setting. Although midwifery resists established medicine in many ways, it is still part of a larger society that respects and uses traditional medical practices. Midwives feel that in order to provide adequate care to their families in all situations, they must be able to interface and deal with the medical profession. However, this causes midwives to be confronted with the same characteristics of the medical industry that they are trying to avoid. By seeking support from the home birth community, licensed, traditional midwives attempt to find a common ground between a complete acceptance of and a complete resistance to the medical establishment that allows them to provide the best possible care to their families.